Doing Anti-Racist Business: Dislodging and Dismantling Racism with 4Reals

In this era of unceasing racialized terror, many question, "How do I become an anti-racist both at home and on the job?" More than a how-to manual, *Doing Anti-Racist Business* utilizes theoretical frameworks and real-life scenarios to provide readers with practical strategies for dismantling racism in the workplace and beyond. Drawing from their unique cultural, vocational, and racial backgrounds, Beckford and Ledder challenge us all to move beyond excuses and enact REAL anti-racist change that can alter business practices for generations to come.

> — **Gregory C. Ellison II, Ph.D.,** Founder and Executive Director of Fearless Dialogues and Associate Professor of Pastoral Care and Counseling at Emory University's Candler School of Theology

Praise for Anti-Racism 4REALS endorsements:

"*Anti-Racism 4REALS* is an intense yet insightful read! Discovering how certain words and actions can unknowingly perpetrate racism and making a conscious decision to change them are essential components to building an anti-racist culture. This book helps you learn how to take the big and small steps need to do this important work.

> — **Leah Gunning Francis, Ph.D.,** author of *Ferguson and Faith: Sparking Leadership and Awakening Community* and featured in documentaries *Ferguson Rises* and *The Talk: Race in America*

"*Anti-Racism 4REALS* is an indispensable resource for equipping all who are serious about the work of dismantling racism. It provides a disciplined approach to generating meaningful engagement that will lead to transformative action. Readers of this excellent book will benefit immensely from their journey."

> — **Dr. Richard Hayes,** Executive Director, Institute of Innovation and Entrepreneurship, Assistant Professor of Management and Entrepreneurship, Hofstra University

"Beckford and Ledder do an incredibly amazing job unpacking complicated concepts and teasing out the nuances – so that readers are provided with the tools they need to be effective agents of change in progressively addressing and dismantling the system of white domination and superiority in all spheres of the human endeavor."

> — **Dr. Herron Keyon Gaston, J.D.**, author of *Let's Talk Race, Diversity, Equity, and Inclusion,* and *The Darkest Night: An Incarceration Memoir, from Jail to Yale*

"Beckford and Ledder have created a highly accessible resource to help you and your community move beyond polite words to real talk that makes a real difference. In this critical time of real danger and real opportunity, we need to get real."

> — **Brian D. McLaren**, author of *Faith After Doubt*

"*Anti-Racism 4Rreals* offers a practical blueprint for the future of anti-racism work."

> — **Mark Feldmeir**, author of *A House Divided*

DOING ANTI-RACIST BUSINESS

DISLODGING & DISMANTLING RACISM WITH THE 4REALS

SHEILA M. BECKFORD &
E. MICHELLE LEDDER, Ph.D.

chalice
PRESS

ChalicePress.com

Print: 9780827206816
EPUB: 9780827206823
EPDF: 9780827206830

Table of Contents

Acknowledgements

Sheila M. Beckford and E. Michelle Ledder realized, from the time we met, it was inevitable we would do this anti-racist anti-racism work together.

We, 4REALS, would like to acknowledge those who were instrumental in bringing this valuable work to life. The formal and informal legal, publishing, accounting, and editorial support we have received throughout this project has helped us in numerous ways to bring this work to fruition. A special mention to Ms. Katara Patton, who edited this and our first book, Anti-Racism 4REALS, going above and beyond by learning and honoring our writing style and anti-racism method. We are grateful.

Sheila M. Beckford

I would like to thank **my ancestors** who nurtured this passion for justice within me.

My mother, "the Diva," **Greta C. Beckford**, taught me to be a person who lives in my truth and not up to others' expectations of me. You taught me that community is essential to ensuring justice and freedom reign. Your spirit lives within me. Thank you, Mami!

Dr. Vincent Harding, one of my mentors, helped me to better understand and offered me an insightful perspective into the work of the Civil Rights Movement. Your patience and corrective measures were filled with the love of a father and a friend.

I will forever love you both and hope to make you proud. Rest in Power!

To **Cheyenne** and **Zai**, I do this work now to ensure a more just world for you to navigate.

To my bestie, **Dana Richardson**, for doing this work from the inside, which brings about REAL cultural change.

E. Michelle Ledder

To the **innumerable Black people and others who have been direct targets of racism**, who have shared their lives and experiences with me, in front of me, and in public spaces. All of what I know about anti-racism has come from BIPAL people. I am indebted beyond measure—and work so that what I do reflects this with integrity.

To **Dr. Eric Severson**, thank you for creating spaces for me to recognize myself as a scholar in my own right. You are the first white person I saw doing anti-racism work explicitly and honorably, and it was at that moment I recognized my life's work.

To **Dr. Teresa Fry Brown**, words could never be enough to express my gratitude to you and for you. Thank you for modeling what it looks like to stare racism and other oppressions right in the face, rebuke them, and retain ALL of your dignity. May the work I do and the way I do it honor you and your legacy.

To **Danyel Iesha Renee Currie**, your life and story echo in every anti-racism resource, workshop, chapter, and project I produce. I will never forget you, nor what you suffered, resisted, and reclaimed. May this and all other work I do honor your memory without disappointment.

4REALS

To **Dr. Leslie Duroseau** and **Dr. Gregory Ellison**, who helped to name us and our project. We recognized more fully who we could become because you saw what we did not yet see. Your guidance and care-filled words of encouragement, insight, and creativity helped to elevate 4REALS to new heights. We are so grateful to walk alongside you both and are excited for what the future holds.

This book is dedicated to all the BIPAL people who endured (and continue to endure) every racialized microaggression, every racist policy, every expression that conspires to protect the system of racism at your expense.

We do this work so that Liberation will be made REAL.

To the Reader

We thank you for entering into this work
to address racism in very REAL ways.

This book was written with all of you in mind.

We deeply appreciate the on-the-ground wisdom that you,
the reader, bring to this work.

4REALS brings truly anti-racist anti-racism practices to life
with 180 strategies and skills.

You bring the contextual wisdom needed for this work
to become REAL where you are.

Let us enter the not only important but critical work
of doing anti-racist business together with:
REAL TALK with REAL STRATEGIES in REAL TIME for REAL CHANGE.

Introduction

That First Meeting—Racialized Terror, Racial Positionality, Real Anti-Racism

In May 2019, Sheila M. Beckford and E. Michelle Ledder met for the first time in the aftermath of racialized terror. The circumstances were unusual but not unique. A prominent, mostly white social justice board of directors had gathered at a retreat center in Maryland—but not for the reasons one might first imagine. Earlier that year, one of its white directors had perpetrated a series of racist acts upon Black people who had gathered at a national conference to oppose social oppression of another group. The board convened in May to address what had happened and to figure out what they needed to do to repair their reputation and "become anti-racist." The fallout of the incidents had been wide and swift. Local branches of Black and Latino/x caucuses had publicly denounced the social justice group and declared unapologetically that they would no longer work with them. The publicity of this explicit break in working relationship, as well as the details and whispers of the racism enacted, sent waves of public judgment upon the social justice group, which was otherwise known for its LGBTQIA full-inclusion activism.

Beckford, a Black woman and chair of the New York Black Caucus, was one of the Black people who was targeted by the racist acts. She was there to provide her testimony, to name exactly what happened as one way to challenge the board of directors to deal directly with what they had done. Ledder, a white woman and director of equity and anti-racism for a global agency on race, was there to highlight the racism and the effects of the racism brought forward from Beckford's and other Black leaders' experiences. Beckford and Ledder named racism in straightforward ways—Beckford as a Black woman who was targeted by and has fought against racism her whole life, and Ledder as a white woman who was there to teach the white board members the specifics of the racism they enacted and a way toward becoming an anti-racist organization. What began as a one-time dialogue about racism with a social justice board of directors turned into an ongoing friendship and working partnership that highlights honest, insightful, and incisive conversations and workshops about racism and anti-racism.

Unfortunately, the above scenario represents not an anomaly but instead one pervasive form of racism—that which stems from organizations that are social justice-based and companies that are white-dominant in leadership, content, and strategy. Claiming to be anti-oppressive, diverse, or inclusive, even for nonprofit or justice-focused groups, does not immunize people or organizations from perpetrating or being targeted by racism. Leadership positions do not miraculously create leaders with the know-how and skill sets to create racial equity and justice. In other words, anti-racism doesn't happen by chance, even in justice-centered organizations—perhaps especially there.

WRITE, DRAW, OR NOTE YOUR RESPONSES: *What were your initial responses to reading that a white leader of a social justice organization perpetrated racialized terror against Black people? Were you surprised? Not surprised? Why?*

We understandably want our jobs and work environments to be places where racism no longer exists, where people can fully and authentically thrive without the policies or practices of white supremacy. We want healthy work environments focused on the skills and work product of employees versus workplace stereotypes that prevent growth and advancement. Anti-racism work environments refuse to allow:

- Implicit bias around first language and accents to disqualify Latino/x employees from certain positions

- "Model minority" racism to harm people of Asian and Pacific Islander racial identities

- Black and Indigenous people to be stereotyped as lazy, Black men as aggressive, or Black women as angry

- A white person's whiteness to qualify them for leadership

When racialized stereotypes of any kind inhabit the minds of leaders and infiltrate "best practices," it is impossible to be doing anti-racist business. No matter how many focus groups gather across lines of racial difference to discuss "diversity" or build relationships, companies will miss the mark. Even reminders to remain cordial, respectful, or professional in an effort to create workplace harmony, in many cases, will perpetuate racism when enacted in the midst of racialized harm. Fortunately, we need not rid ourselves of the best of best practices or our business sense to do the work of anti-racism. What we need are anti-racism tools and interpretive lenses to help us see *how* best practices and business sense can be utilized to lead us directly and responsibly into anti-racism work and growth.

One foundational lens necessary for anti-racism work but often ignored in the business world is racial positionality.[1] Diversity and inclusion often teach a model of equality that flattens out differences to highlight our similarities. However, the realities of race and racism create different consequences for people based on racial markers. Within the system of racism, white people are prioritized, privileged, and protected, while BIPAL (Black, Indigenous, Pacific Islander, Asian, and Latino/x)[2] people are dehumanized, disenfranchised, and discriminated against. Just like diverse business models consider pathways to success through different perspectives, focus areas, and wisdom based on their ideologies, so also do we, based on our racialized contextual realities. Racial positionality signifies the very real but symbolic spheres within which BIPAL people and white people exist within the system of racism. In other words, the term helps us keep in the forefront how people of different races experience the world differently because of racism. Organizations often get anti-racism work wrong because they attempt to use a language of equality (similarity) to discuss, describe, and dismantle a system based in difference. What we need are words and actions that retain the ideal of equality while addressing the realities of difference inherent in the system of racism.

---

[1] E. Michelle Ledder first used the term *racial positionality* to describe racial identity within the system of racism while working at the General Commission on Religion and Race (GCORR) (2016 to 2021). While she hadn't heard the term *racial positionality* before, it entered her thinking emerging from concepts and pedagogies taught to her by her doctoral adviser, Dr. Teresa Fry Brown.

[2] Many articles reference People of Color (PoC) to avoid centering whiteness when describing racial identity. Others utilize the term BIPOC (Black, Indigenous, and People of Color) to do the same while also identifying the harm which Black and Indigenous people experience at the hands of other People of Color. Sheila M. Beckford uses the term BIPAL (Black, Indigenous, Pacific Islanders, Asian, and Latino/x) to represent multiple racial identities by naming them separately to further decenter whiteness in discussions of anti-racism and beyond.

White people are crying out more and more, "What can I do?" But they are in deep need of anti-racist strategies that do not perpetrate racism. BIPAL people need strategies to combat the inherent consequences of racism—interpersonal and institutional racism, internalized racism—and strategies for how to hold white "allies" accountable without capitulating to racist ideologies. In such a time as this, it is increasingly necessary to provide models and options for anti-racism that refuse to rely on temporary fixes. We believe that *Doing Anti-Racist Business: Dislodging and Dismantling Racism with the 4REALS* is one model capable of moving ethical and good-intended people from "thoughts and prayers" to the real strategies that bring about real change in real time.

What We Need is Real Talk, Not More Talk, about Racism and Anti-Racism

Many businesses that want to include anti-racism work focus on dialogues. We want to talk *with* one another instead of *at* one another. We want to understand each other better. We want to unlock that which we don't know in order to find the answers we so desperately need. Dialogue in and of itself is not the problem. Dialogues that result only in more talk are the problem. But what does it mean to have *real talk* about racism and anti-racism versus just *more talk*? We thought we'd put our own work to work by sharing our thoughts with you using the anti-racism foundational lens of racial positionality. What follows are separate responses by Sheila M. Beckford and E. Michelle Ledder. Each of us will not only respond based in our racial positionality but also make the connections between what we say and our racial positionality as clear as possible. The reasoning for this is multifold: It helps us, as writers, keep our own racial positionality at the forefront, which helps us to do anti-racism work well; it helps to create clear connections for you, the reader, between anti-racism work and racial identity; and it foreshadows the structure of the book ahead.

So, let's try it. The prompt is this: What does it mean to have REAL TALK, not more talk, about racism and anti-racism?

BECKFORD'S RESPONSE: In the Black community, the phrase *REAL TALK* means giving it to you straight with no filter, no hiding behind respectability politics or politeness. Respectability politics occurs when BIPAL people are directed by those in their same group to assimilate to the dominant group in order to be accepted. We are told that if we just follow the rules, get our education, dress well, and speak well, we will be protected from harm by white wrath. For example, recently someone shared a meme. The top photo included the Rev. Dr. Martin Luther King Jr., Rev. Ralph Abernathy, and others marching arm in arm, dressed in suits and trench coats. The image on the bottom of the meme featured young men wearing pants that sagged. In between the two images a caption read, "They respected this [the top image] and not this." My REAL TALK response beneath the post stated, "The Reverend Dr. Martin Luther King Jr. was assassinated anyhow."

In the spring of 2020, the world viewed the murders of Ahmaud Arbery (Georgia) and George Floyd (Minnesota). We were infuriated by the killings of Breonna Taylor (Kentucky) and Elijah McClain (Colorado). In response, white people sought ways to understand their own racism. Many sought answers by reading books, while others sought to find the answers by asking (in fact, demanding) for BIPAL people, especially Black people, to educate them. Although some of the materials were great reads and allowed people to form book studies, they lacked something essential; their talk remained just that: talk. BIPAL, especially Black and Indigenous people, are tired of talk without change. We are tired of hearing talk that leads to more talk but not to action. REAL TALK requires action.

Businesses need REAL TALK, not more talk. While working in a predominantly white institution, a white person made the following statement: "I don't see your color." Immediately, I corrected her, saying, "I am a big, tall, Black woman with an afro; you better see my color." I continued to explain to her that to deny seeing my color is called erasure. White people do this to erase the part of a person that makes them uncomfortable in an effort to feel comfortable with an individual or group. Of course, this interruption of her racist statement made her and other white people in the room uncomfortable because they had never experienced REAL TALK. Many white people who were there spoke with me after the meeting, and for months afterward shared with me their displeasure at my public response. They told me I should have educated her without publicly embarrassing her. More talk pulls white people to the side to discuss their racism in private. REAL TALK interrupts harm in the moment. More talk allows people to remain where they are. REAL TALK requires action steps, such as white people holding each other accountable for their racism. More talk may show intellectual "wokeness" but no reparative actions. REAL TALK calls for change in behavior reinforced by anti-racist policies. More talk promotes harm; REAL TALK interrupts harm.

> ### *More talk promotes harm*
> ### *REAL TALK interrupts harm*

LEDDER'S RESPONSE: For those of us who are white, we are consistent in finding ways to distract ourselves from having to do our hard work of anti-racism. Having more talk about racism and anti-racism instead of REAL TALK is one such diversion. The reasons for this abound and, at this point, don't matter. The outcome is that, in terms of anti-racism work, those of us who are white must develop the capability and the motivation to reduce our racism, which pries our attention and energy away from anti-racist strategies. Ironically, avoiding REAL TALK by using dialogue is one distraction.

One way white people misinterpret, misuse, and misappropriate anti-racism strategies created by BIPAL people is by co-opting dialogues. Whether dialogues are in the form of book studies, workshops/trainings, small group conversations, or relationship building over food, those of us who are white consistently use these opportunities for more talk rather than REAL TALK about racism and anti-racism. We do this in numerous ways, including but not limited to the following:

- **We take up all the space in conversations.** White people will fill the space of anti-racism talk with our experiences, our feelings, and our strategies. We either feel too uncomfortable to deal with our own culpability or too inadequate to do something meaningful, and to compensate, we fill the space with our words. The white supremacist notion that white people's ideas and feelings should fill any and all spaces (even those dedicated to anti-racism) perpetrates racism with more talk.

- **We create talk "about" racism/anti-racism without action.** Have you ever attended a meeting that gathers solely to discuss the previous meeting without providing next steps or new ideas? In anti-racism work, this translates to book studies that lead to discussions but not to action; workshop hoarding that makes those of us who are white feel better but that does nothing to change our methods or behavior; or quoting facts about racism (or anti-racism strategies) without enacting them in tangible, meaningful, or powerful ways according to BIPAL people. More talk.

- **We develop our own anti-racism task forces or strategies.** When those of us who are white create our own anti-racism strategies, without taking our guidance from BIPAL people, we only create more talk. We are duplicating (badly) the efforts of BIPAL people who already have strategies in place that we can learn to support responsibly. When white people believe we are the ones to create anti-racism strategies, we perpetrate the racism that teaches us that white people always have the answer. More subtle excuses for this racism sound like "I want to use my position of power to create change" or "I wanted to do the proper research for a sound course of action."

REAL TALK is always anti-racist—it *actually* interrupts and dismantles racism. More talk about racism and anti-racism reifies the status quo and generates new expressions of racism all the while. For example, REAL TALK implores those of us who are white to utilize the book study to enact the anti-racism strategies that emerge from its pages. REAL TALK is also anti-racist in **both** content and method. More talk can be anti-racist in one while perpetrating racism in another. For example, attending a protest against police brutality against Black people is anti-racist in content. White people attending the protest and talking to reporters instead of guiding them toward Black activists is racist in method.

ACTION-NOW Learning Engagement:

SCENARIO: A group of MBA students got together to devise a way that they could be savvy in business dealings while retaining humane relationships with each other and business partners. They crafted a set of policies and parameters for negotiating financial deals, but they were stuck on how to address conflict. They had been well-schooled in the ways of gaining advantage, of loopholes, and of dog-eat-dog interactions. This group, however, wanted to create ways of relating with people and businesses that honored the humanity of people, including themselves. After an hour of brainstorming, one of the senior students stood to speak, sharing her paraphrase of a very old story she thought would resonate with what they were trying to achieve.

She said, "If someone wrongs you, go and correct them when you are alone together. If they listen to you, you can work it out together without the group having to get in your business. But if they won't listen, take with you two or three others so you'll have witnesses present. But if they still won't pay attention, you'll have no recourse but to report the wrongdoing before the whole community. Then, the group can figure out what to do."

When people spend any amount of time together, there will be conflict. It's one thing to address the wrongdoing with no regard for the one who has caused the harm. It's cutthroat, it's "just business," or we claim to "do what we have to do." It's another when the goal is to both address the problem and hold onto the personal or business relationships with the culprit.

The scenario above is based in a very old story, one told to generations of people who seek solutions to a very old problem. But it sounds familiar, doesn't it? How many times have we been told to address sensitive matters in private, not to air out the company's dirty laundry, or to address problems that happen in meetings with the person individually rather than "reply all" to the email?

For a moment—think about the BEST way to address someone who has wronged you at work. Consider how you will address this person who is more than simply a fellow employee; this person is your managing supervisor. When you learn that your manager has done something with negative consequences for you, how would you address it while keeping in mind the power dynamics at play? Write your first thoughts here:

Many of us would immediately think to speak with our manager in private, to discuss the situation with each other to work it out before any actions were taken in public. The old story shared by the MBA student rings true for many of us.

Beckford's response earlier noted that often in anti-racism work, talk gets REAL when racism is called out in the moment. It matters not whether the racism is considered blatant or subtle; the white person who is made aware of their racism becomes embarrassed or ashamed and reacts. Placing the burden of responsibility on the person who named the racism rather than the one who perpetrated it, the story about taking the wrong-doer aside in private is interpreted to mean that the "calling out of racism" should also be done in private. While there might be scenarios when this course of action is best, it creates harm in anti-racism work. This is because the above story refers to a wrongdoing that has occurred between only two people. "If someone wrongs you..." Racism enacted in front of others has happened in public. The harm has already been done against BIPAL people, and, REAL TALK: The only people who probably aren't aware of it are the white people. Thus, the call for a private consult over someone's racism is invoked to protect white people's feelings. (Sometimes, BIPAL people invoke this too—part of the reason is that internalized racism teaches BIPAL people to want to protect white people's feelings!)

We'll be focusing on practicing examples of how to interrupt racism in the REAL TIME chapter, but for now, how does the reinterpretation of the "take the wrongdoer aside in private" story help you understand how REAL TALK can be used to interrupt racism in the moment and why it's important? How does your racial identity influence how you're thinking about this right now?

Chapter 1:

4REALS: Real Talk with Real Strategies in Real Time for Real Change

Anti-Racism 4REALS is both an anti-racist template and an anti-racism organization. The term *anti-racism* assumes as true the reality of racism's ability to survive and thrive in environments if there are not intentional and explicit actions and actors capable of disrupting, dismantling, and destroying it. Racism will not surrender to the weak calls for gradual change that are beholden to the timeline of those who are racially protected. Rather, racism is fortified by such efforts—it relishes in its ability to bathe in the tepid waters of compromise and consciences that are comfortable with accepting the suffering of others as collateral damage. Anti-racism is anything that *actually* interrupts and dismantles racism.

> ### *Anti-Racism is anything that ACTUALLY interrupts and dismantles racism*

The question is, how do we do that? Anti-Racism 4REALS literally suggests four (4) REALS.

In this book, we will employ several strategies and approaches to developing REAL TALK about racism, which ultimately means action and change. The following describes the components of this book and what to expect as you work through it.

REAL TALK finds every way possible to use words to interrupt and dismantle racism. Have you ever been part of discussions about racism and anti-racism that are so shallow and superficial that you might as well have been talking about the weather or the local sports team? There are many conversations that never get to what is needed to interrupt and dismantle racism. Even dialogues with titles that include words like *diversity, racial justice, racial reconciliation* (whatever that's supposed to mean!), or *anti-racism* can fall short when they do not get at what needs to be said and how it needs to be said.

The corporate world teaches its leaders to speak in neutral terms to maintain professionalism. Schools hide behind political correctness, which allows false objectivity to masquerade as facts. Government agencies rely on protocols vetted by strict meritocracy ideals, as if implicit bias has no influence on explicit interpretations or decisions. Nonprofits often equate the good work for which their organization was founded as a false immunity to perpetrating inequity. Even those who rely on interpersonal relationship standards such as remaining "polite," "nice," "patient," "empathetic," or "compassionate," fail hard. It's one thing for institutions to prioritize profits or purpose over people, but how is it possible that these good-sounding words do harm?

The problems are not with the terms or inclinations themselves but with how they are interpreted and lived out while addressing oppression—in this case, racism. For example, *polite* and *nice* become code words for, "Don't say anything that gets white people upset." *Patient* transforms into soft-pedaling around difficult issues rather than directly naming them. *Empathetic* translates to understanding racism as someone's opinion or upbringing rather than addressing the oppression and injustice. *Compassionate* is described as "meeting the people where they are" but ends up leaving racists where they are until they feel comfortable enough to change, if ever. (By the way, if that last sentence was difficult for you to read, it may be because you've been hearing more talk about racism versus anti-racist REAL TALK. We'll go into this more throughout the book!)

REAL TALK not only names racism directly but also says things in ways that enact anti-racist strategies within the content and proclamation of the words themselves. For example, in contrast to "journey language," REAL TALK advocates for "entry point" language.[3] Entry points create a way for all people to start anti-racism work right now. The work of an anti-racism trainer, book, or workshop is to find entry points for people and develop learning engagements that connect someone's entry point (perspective, prior training, learning style, and so on) with the work of anti-racism. Entry point language also removes the literal and symbolic space for people (especially white people) to wiggle out of responsibilities to dismantle racism that journey language permits. REAL TALK places what is needed for discussions about racism and anti-racism in direct contact with how to say the uncomfortable things, how to do the uncomfortable things, and how to remain responsible and humane all the while.

REAL STRATEGIES prioritize ACTION-NOW Learning Engagements to move everyone beyond just talking about racism to taking immediate anti-

---

[3] E. Michelle Ledder first used "entry point" language to describe places where people do the work of anti-racism while she was working at the General Commission on Religion and Race (GCORR) (2016 to 2021).

racism actions. Rather than relying on models that demand that talk (REAL or otherwise) occur first and in isolation from action, REAL STRATEGIES place action at the center of Anti-Racism 4REALS. If anti-racism is anything that *actually* interrupts and dismantles racism, it just makes sense that actions are necessary. However, so much of current anti-racism practice is predicated on talking about and agreeing on truth of content, strategies necessary, and course of actions in order to engage. Book studies abound as new information is published and groups gather in unprecedented numbers after the racialized-terror-murders of George Floyd, Ahmaud Arbery, Breonna Taylor, and Elijah McClain in 2019 and 2020. But how many of those book studies have created any change, let alone sustainable change, for racial justice or equity? How many book studies have created tangible, meaningful, and powerful anti-racism acts? If we are really honest, how many book studies led to quoting truths *about* racism and anti-racism without *actually* interrupting and dismantling racism?

ACTION-NOW Learning Engagements are exercises that bridge the gap between learning about something and doing something. Anti-Racism 4REALS believes that all people can begin doing anti-racism immediately. REAL STRATEGIES interrupt and dismantle the workshop-hoarder mentality that believes attending workshops can be equated with anti-racism work or that one more workshop will "get me ready" to do what's necessary. REAL STRATEGIES also break the chains of information-only workshops—even at the introductory entry point—by creating processes by which action can be taken right now. For example, have you ever been in the presence of someone making a racist joke? How did you respond? Did you interrupt them? Did you stay silent? Did you leave? Did you laugh? REAL STRATEGIES moves from learning and talking about anti-racism work to the actual doing of reparative racial justice.

REAL STRATEGIES are placed at the end of every chapter—including the introduction—so that the work of anti-racism begins without a waiting period. Each will be based on a three-part template of THE BIG IDEA (what you learn about in the chapter), ACTION-NOW (for immediate use), and ENTRY POINTS (racial positionality and prior skill set). Without REAL STRATEGIES, even the realest of REAL TALK becomes just more talk. Book studies that have the potential to dismantle racist thinking will lead to actual anti-racist acts instead of dialogues about the dialogues. Missed opportunities to interrupt racism will decrease as we learn how information becomes the actions that bolster our courage, resistance, and conviction. REAL STRATEGIES make REAL TALK real.

REAL TIME incorporates role-playing scenarios so that people can practice scripts and rehearse plans to prepare to interrupt and dismantle racism in the moment. REAL TALK and REAL STRATEGIES can't interrupt and dismantle racism if we can't enact them when the racism occurs. Racism happens in real time, so anti-racism must also happen in REAL TIME. Anti-Racism 4REALS recognizes that even prepared anti-racists will experience situations when racism occurs and the words or interruptions won't come. This is for many reasons. Sometimes, for those of us who are white, the momentum of our inaction has yet to be overcome, or we recognize the racism but don't have a skill set necessary to interrupt it or dismantle it. For BIPAL people, at times the act of racism itself is so hurtful that the trauma of the event necessitates self-care without overt disruption. Sometimes, BIPAL people wait for white people to step up and take responsibility for practicing the anti-racism they purport to be about. At other times, internalized oppression creates in BIPAL people the need to protect white people or shield them from their own embarrassment—even as they perpetrate racism.

But REAL TIME isn't restricted to racism that occurs "out there." 4REALS, as an organization, believes that anti-racism isn't simply information that is taught, it is the method by which the work is done. 4REALS believes that REAL TIME begins in the learning (even during anti-racism workshops or books) and that there are conscientious ways to address racism even at the introductory entry points. Interrupting racism in anti-racism workshops has the power to model what it looks and sounds like when best business practices meet ethical humanity and anti-racism in REAL TIME. These same strategies can be used to provide a model for interrupting racism in nonprofits, schools, government agencies, corporations, and at home—if not in all settings.

CAUTION: Anti-racists re-enact only the *interruption* of racism, not the racism itself, in role-playing scenarios because this mitigates to the best of our ability the harms of racism. We do not perpetrate racism in real time in order to interrupt racism in REAL TIME. (For white people reading this and wondering how to become better at recognizing racism in real time without role playing it, use a Google search. Unfortunately, plenty of examples of every type of racism abound.)

REAL CHANGE crafts accountability templates and measures to ensure that tangible, meaningful, and powerful change for racial justice replaces good intentions and workshops. REAL CHANGE requires that we focus on outcome, not on intent. There is often a disconnectedness between intent and what actually occurs. One reason for this is racialized implicit bias, but other factors impede REAL CHANGE. Some organizations attempt to do anti-racism work using the "add-on" method, which retains a foundation of white supremacy and "adds" trainings or special days on top. Some leaders are deeply entrenched in the way things are because that's how they got there.

Anti-racism 4REALS defines anti-racism as anything that *actually* interrupts and dismantles racism. REAL CHANGE provides ways to track, assess, and analyze successes and failures (yes, failures) and make on-the-go shifts that avoid the most common roadblocks and obstacles to anti-racism work. REAL CHANGE creates methods of accountability and transparency that build not only timelines and momentum but also trust. *Change* is a word that has been cheapened by superficial and temporary fixes that might feel good to some in the moment but that do nothing to shift the ethos of an institution or the commitment of an individual. REAL CHANGE provides the external measurements and an accountability paradigm that bring all people the opportunity to participate in anti-racism work that actually does the work of anti-racism.

Chapter Outline: Two Responses and an ACTION-NOW Learning Engagement

Beckford and Ledder have created a way to model what REAL TALK with REAL STRATEGIES in REAL TIME about racism and anti-racism can mean for REAL CHANGE. Each chapter will highlight one REAL and will include three sub-sections: a response from Beckford, a response from Ledder, and a collective response based in an anti-racist skill/action the reader can use right away. In-book journaling with prompt questions (as you've already seen) creates the literal space for any reader to move beyond just absorbing material to internalizing the work necessary for anti-racism.

The chapter on REAL TALK focuses on the role of silence in its multiple forms—repressive or oppressive, vigilant or violent, protective or as a means of survival. The REAL STRATEGIES chapter highlights how racial positionality influences which actions white "allies" and BIPAL people should engage. Included also is a chart with nine sets of scenarios and multiple entry points for immediate use. REAL TIME gets right to the point, prioritizing doing the work of interrupting and dismantling racism and the obstructions that get in the way. Chapter 4 on REAL CHANGE includes a list of things anti-racists should stop doing right now as well as accountability measures and templates for anti-racist outcomes. Finally, the conclusion presents an overarching anti-racism strategy that honors racial positionality and creates a method for challenging white people to do the anti-racism work needed without placing a double burden on BIPAL people.

ACTION-NOW Learning Engagement: Doing Anti-Racism Work Responsibly

Anti-Racism 4REALS believes at every moment, every person can do anti-racism work. This is why we've included critical journal prompts even in the introduction and why now we're providing an ACTION-NOW Learning

Engagement highlighting an anti-racism strategy you can use as soon as you read it: an Anti-Racist Pledge.[4]

An Anti-Racist Pledge can be seen as corrections to safe space or even brave space agreements: lists of agreed-upon ways of speaking and being with one another when having difficult conversations or working alongside each other across lines of difference. Safe space agreements attempted to create literal spaces where people felt safe enough to be vulnerable with others who are different from themselves. Soon, however, critiques of these attempts emerged as participants realized it was impossible to create full safety. Brave space agreements attempt to rectify this by replacing the impossible goal of safety with the possibility of creating spaces where people could be brave enough to be vulnerable even though 100 percent safety couldn't be achieved. Both safe space and brave space agreements fall into the same trap, however: They still prioritize the dominant or protected group.

Racism works just like all other spheres of oppression. Within a system of oppression, there are those who are protected, prioritized, and privileged, and those who are discriminated against and who are the direct targets of the oppression. Within the system of racism, white people are the protected group and BIPAL people are the direct targets. More than the inability of any list to provide 100 percent safety, the limitations of safe space and brave space agreements lie in their replication of the dominant group's worldview and the protection of their safety and comfort. Here, we're including three anti-racist pledges so that you, the reader, can start doing REAL TALK the very next time your anti-racism group/workshop leader initiates an agreement to determine how the work will proceed.

The following table has three columns. The first represents the objective of the pledge. The second column represents how you might see it written in a safe space or brave space agreement. The final column shows language for an anti-racist pledge. Outcomes are listed for the safe/brave space item and the anti-racist item. Notice how the outcomes of the safe/brave space items get away from the stated objective while the anti-racist pledges point more closely toward it. Notice your reactions to reading them. If you are white, take special care to think about how the safe/brave space item has protected you in the past. If you are a BIPAL person, think about how, if at all, the anti-racist

[4]E. Michelle Ledder first created a version of the Anti-Racist Pledge while working at the General Commission on Religion and Race (GCORR). The first versions were inspired by attending a meeting hosted by the Young People's Department of the Washington, D.C., NAACP, who introduced a dialogue agreement created by groups caucused by race. The current version included here has been adapted and modified by 4REALS: Anti-Racist Anti-Racism Training and Consulting LLC.

pledge item would mitigate the harm of the falsely named safe/brave spaces you've been part of in the past. If you believe it wouldn't, what language would help it to do that? For everyone, name at least one specific thing you can do to live out one of the anti-racist pledge items the next time you are doing anti-racist work.

OBJECTIVE	SAFE/BRAVE SPACE AGREEMENT	ANTI-RACIST PLEDGE
Recognize that everyone comes to anti-racism work from different experiences.	Assume everyone has good intentions. (Outcome: White people believe that intent erases harm done by racism.)	Assume humanity/build trust. (Outcome: Everyone's humanity is assumed to be true; but white people recognize it is their job to always be working to build the trust necessary for BIPAL people to be vulnerable about race/racism with them; white people never expect to be trusted just because they are in an anti-racism space.)
Anti-racism work is hard and will probably be uncomfortable at least some of the time.	Be challenged to be uncomfortable. (Outcome: Experiences of discomfort between BIPAL people and white people are flattened as if the harm from racism is the same as that of the growing awareness of responsibility for perpetrating it.)	Do our own work and take on intentional challenges. (Outcome: Everyone will be challenged in different ways depending on their racial positionality; BIPAL people might be challenged to trust that anything will change by engaging anti-racism work with white people, while white people will be challenged to take responsibility for their racism without demanding that BIPAL people care for them.)
Treat one another with dignity and respect while working through the realities of racism and responsibilities for anti-racism.	Be polite and respect one another. (Outcome: People use "good-sounding" words to silence resistance or challenges to racism; or REAL TALK is silenced for just "more talk.")	Recognize and avoid using "good-sounding" words that actually do harm: that is, civil, polite, calm, and even nonviolence in some cases. (Outcome: More REAL TALK and less "more talk.")

FOR WHITE PEOPLE: How has one item from the safe/brave space agreement specifically protected you in anti-racism spaces in the past?

FOR BIPAL PEOPLE: How, if at all, would an anti-racist pledge from the chart specifically mitigate the harm a falsely named safe/brave space item has done? If not at all, what language would you change?

FOR ALL: How, specifically, will you enact one anti-racist pledge item from the chart?

Chapter 2:

REAL TALK

The first of the four REALS, REAL TALK, has been defined as that which finds every way possible to use words to interrupt and dismantle racism. REAL TALK not only names racism directly, but also says things in ways that enact anti-racist strategies within the content and proclamation of the words themselves. REAL TALK creates opportunities for every person to engage in anti-racism right away. It places what is needed for discussions about racism and anti-racism in direct contact with how to say the uncomfortable things, how to do the uncomfortable things, and how to remain responsible and humane all the while.

In this chapter, we'll delve more deeply into REAL TALK by focusing on the anti-racism reality that "silence is violence." Our racially positioned responses will include REAL TALK in at least three ways: [1] REAL TALK about "silence is violence" as an anti-racism strategy; [2] REAL TALK about how racism co-opts "silence is violence" to perpetrate more racism; and [3] how REAL TALK can be used to help all of us do anti-racism work by considering a "horizon of silence" as the foundation for this chapter's ACTION-NOW Learning Engagement. Let's begin...

BECKFORD'S RESPONSE: Before you go any further, take a moment to think about your organization's no-tolerance-for-violence policy.

WRITE YOUR RESPONSE BELOW: *What definitions or words come to mind while reflecting on your organization's no-tolerance-for-violence policy?*

Organizations institute no-tolerance-for-violence policies and enforce them with rigorous punishments. School systems suspend or expel students, while employers terminate employees. However, these same institutions' best practices protect and perpetuate violence through silence. Have you ever heard the phrase "silence is violence," or "white silence is racial violence?"

In many instances, when white people witness racialized terror enacted against their Black, Indigenous, Pacific Islander, Asian, and Latino/x colleagues—especially their Black and Indigenous colleagues—they are silent until there is an opportunity to speak with the target one-on-one. This is the time when they express how the act was "wrong" or how the tone or rhetoric spewed was offensive *even* to them. However, they were silent at the moment because it was beneficial to remain in the system.

In his book study, Dr. Walter Brueggemann highlights how silence can perpetrate violence within organizational systems: "Silence is a complex matter. It can refer to awe before unutterable holiness, but it can also refer to coercion where some voices are silenced in the interest of control by the dominant voices."[5] Brueggemann refers to this as "repressive silence."

When a BIPAL person offers an opinion, strategy, or perspective, repressive silence dismisses it until their white counterpart offers support or repeats it almost verbatim as if it were their own. The consequences of this then pile up. BIPAL people offer ideas that are consistently knocked down or undervalued. Then, BIPAL people begin to feel knocked down and undervalued. As a result, BIPAL people question the value of sharing ideas knowing they will be forced into repressive silence.

Pay attention to the voices that are listened to and valued within your company. If you recognize this dynamic occurring in team meetings, notice who is speaking and who is not. (Do not use this awareness strategy to retaliate against BIPAL people who are silent or have stopped contributing ideas, but to identify whether your company perpetrates racism in this way.)

Many organizations believe in establishing diversity and inclusion hiring practices in an attempt to solve this problem. However, merely employing BIPAL managers without addressing racism replicates the current culture. Selection for these leadership positions often requires BIPAL people to deny our cultures and assimilate into the dominant white group.

Some examples are quite subtle. Consider the business that hires people who are "moldable." The focus is placed not on one's skills but rather on the extent to which the company can create (or mold) the employee to match the

---

[5]Walter Brueggemann, *Interrupting Silence: God's Command to Speak Out* (Louisville, KY: Westminster John Knox Press, 2018), 1.

desired organizational culture. To many, this strategy creates "culture fit" and "employee unity." Yet this dynamic is often used as a tool of repressive silence. Requiring that someone be "moldable," rather than allowing for flexibility, is business jargon for promoting assimilation.

Molding encourages group thinking. Groupthink encourages oppression because of its requirement to accept whatever policies and practices are in place. If you are reading this with a commitment to do anti-racism work, but your business uses terms like "molding," "culture fit," or "groupthink," your efforts may contradict themselves.

The aforementioned terms give some BIPAL people pause when applying for positions. Depending on the racial identity of the BIPAL person, the response can be different. However, in some BIPAL communities these are buzz words that have been included in "the talk" and signal us not to apply.

WRITE YOUR RESPONSE: *Without googling or using any other resource, explain your understanding of "the talk" on the lines below.*

_____

_____

_____

_____

_____

_____

_____

"The talk" is the epitome of REAL TALK, which occurs when Black families send their children into the world. "The talk" is a protective measure with specific strategies meant to ensure Black children's survival in a white supremacist world. It caters to white people's expectations of Black submissiveness. The business world has co-opted "the talk" not to help Black people's survival but to coerce silence:

- "Work twice as hard"
- "Do not be too loud"
- "Do not show anger or aggression"
- "Be yourself" (REAL TALK translation: "Be an impostor")

We are called to ignore our culture and our experiences or to die to oneself to fit in. When any aspect of BIPAL communities' culture is introduced, it is often met with inappropriate expressions of curiosity or disdain. Human resources departments are trained to gaslight and deflect any racialized related trauma reported by BIPAL people. As a result, our experiences, voices, and authenticity are repressed.

In the corporate world, anti-Blackness is pervasive, accepted, and enforced through policies and hiring practices. Recently, Wells Fargo's CEO said that the difficulty of hiring Black employees stems from a "limited pool of Black talent."[6] While the news media picked up this story, causing the CEO to apologize for his "insensitive comment reflecting my own unconscious bias," the fallout was minimal. Why? Because it echoes the prevalent culture among corporations.

What often goes unreported are the ways the term "unconscious bias" is used as a euphemism to disguise racism and is embedded in policies and employee manuals. For example, grooming, attire, and hygiene standards restrict some cultural hairstyles and attire. Strict dress codes are a way to discriminate against BIPAL people without stating the obvious requirement to meet white standards. Although much of the racism stems from the company's ethos, many businesses treat racialized terror as isolated incidents rather than a systemic problem.

Throughout this book, we will reinforce that the only way to dislodge, disrupt, and dismantle racism is to interrupt it in **REAL TIME**, which includes speaking out and challenging silence. But **REAL TALK**: What if I told you that those of us who are Black, Indigenous, Pacific Islanders, Asian, and Latino/x participate in perpetuating racism by interrupting white protective silence?

The white dominant culture is often told not to speak first while Black and Indigenous people are present because white voices and ideas are often valued over their BIPAL counterparts. But in some cases, when BIPAL people speak first, it primes the conversation, and white thoughts and truths are suppressed, causing racism to hide in plain sight. For example: During an anti-racism training including Black, Indigenous, Asian, Latino/x, and white participants, whenever the facilitator asked a philosophical question, there

---

[6]McEvoy, Jemima. "Wells Fargo CEO Apologizes For Saying There's A 'Limited Pool of Black Talent.'" Forbes. September 23, 2020. https://www.forbes.com/sites/jemimamcevoy/2020/09/23/wells-fargo-ceo-apologizes-for-saying-theres-a-limited-pool-of-black-talent/?sh=483321b14622

https://www.forbes.com/sites/jemimamcevoy/2020/09/23/wells-fargo-ceo-apologizes-for-saying-theres-a-limited-pool-of-black-talent/?sh=63fb44794622.Accessed 8/30/2022.

was an awkward silence. To break the silence, the BI(P)AL[7] participants would respond, and then white people would feel comfortable enough to share their thoughts on the topic. They took their cues on how to react from the BI(P)AL participants.

After witnessing this a few times, one of the facilitators, a white woman, stood up and gave the following instructions: "For the next question, I am going to require all who identify as a person of color, whether Black, Asian, Latino/x, or Indigenous, to respond after our white siblings." The question: "We are asking each of you to name three things of your culture that you take pride in." The white participants responded:

- "I know this may sound offensive, but I take pride in being white."

- "I take pride in my privilege because I can use it to benefit others."

- "I take pride in my heritage."

- "I cannot imagine what being Black feels like, but I do not want to experience it."

The responses went along in that manner.

The facilitator then said, "Okay, now all of my siblings who were asked to be quiet, please respond to the question." The responses included:

- "Dance"

- "Food"

- "Community"

- "Family gatherings"

- "Language"

- "Heritage"

The list continued to build in that manner. Once the facilitator started to list the noticeably different responses, one white woman interjected, "Wait, wait, was this a trick question?" Another white woman chimed in, "That is not the question that was asked of us! Had we known, we would have responded differently."

Right now, before you read anything else, in your opinion, respond to this prompt:

---

[7]Authors use BI(P)AL here to denote that there were no Pacific Islanders in this specific group.

In your opinion, did the facilitator use a trick question? Why or why not? What was your response while reading the comments from our white counterparts?

WRITE YOUR RESPONSE HERE:

The question *was* the same. As a matter of fact, look closely at the invitation given to the BI(P)AL participants to respond to. The question was not posed to the BI(P)AL participants directly. What was different? There was nowhere to hide, and there were no cues to prepare an anti-racist response. The BI(P)AL participants did not provide the white participants with an opportunity to protect or tone down their racism. There were no leading responses for the white participants to use to reshape their thoughts or to shield their racism.

Knowing the difference between when silence is interrupting racism and when it is allowing it to hide in plain sight is often difficult. As BIPAL people, we tend to want to ease the discomfort of white people. We often find ourselves protecting the white dominant group by stating, "Oh, they don't know," or "That is not what they meant," or "They did not understand the question." We further surrogate ourselves by posing an alternate way or rephrasing the question for their understanding and protection.

Approximately two years after this training, a friend and I were discussing this event. Her response surprised me to the point that my eyes widened involuntarily. She stated that when our white siblings began to question whether they were tricked, she felt bad for them and immediately wanted to offer a defense for them. However, before she spoke, she took a moment to replay what had actually occurred. She shared with me her realization that her first impulse was to justify the white people's indignation. Her thought process went like this:

- "First, I thought maybe the question was a trick question."

- "Then I replayed it in my mind." (She placed her hand on her head.)

- "I then realized that it was the same question that we responded to."

- "No! I'm trippin'."

- "I then told the group that I didn't think this was a trick question."

In this follow-up conversation, I realized that white manipulation (fragility)[8] had nearly overridden my friend's own wisdom and the facts! The ideas of the white dominant group had become the litmus test for normalcy. My friend used a process to reclaim her trust in her own instincts—her own eyes, her own ears, and her natural capacity to know the truth.

Silence is violence because the results of repressive or oppressive silence are internalized racism, racism hiding in plain sight, and policies misnamed as if they are anti-racist despite promoting and protecting racism.

LEDDER'S RESPONSE: The phrase "silence is violence" has become almost everyday language since 2020. From anti-racism work to protest signs and activists' challenges to politicians, the phrase evokes action by its reference to inaction. The rhyme scheme flows easily off the tongue and captures the wandering eye of the internet and news media. As a formulation of language itself, it's catchy and powerful. But words are slippery things—they are released into the world with a power of their own, no longer bound to their original authors or speakers.[9] Ironically, as words become more commonplace, it's more important to define and describe what they're meant to do.

---

[8]The term "white manipulation" is used by Sheila M. Beckford to more accurately describe the reality of what is widely referred to as white fragility. According to Beckford, the term *white fragility* centers and recenters whiteness by protecting the racism of white victimhood. In contrast, the term *white manipulation* best describes both the outcome and the strategy. In this book, we use the wording "white manipulation (fragility)" because the term *white fragility* is so widely known that we need a connecting piece to help people know which kind of racism is referred to here.

[9]"Words are slippery things" is a phrase Ledder has heard her former undergrad professor Dr. Eric Severson say many times, though it does not appear in any of his published work. Also see, *Nommo.* "In West Africa, the Dogon people of Mali believe that the African concept of Nommo, the power of the spoken word, carries an energy that produces all life and influences everything from destiny to the naming of children. By human utterance or through the spoken word, human beings can invoke a kind of spiritual power. Nommo, the generative power of the spoken word, is the force that gives life to everything. It is present everywhere, and it brings into existence all that is seen and unseen..." Molefi Kete Asante and Ama Mazama, eds., "Nommo," *Encyclopedia of African Religion*, accessed June 20, 2021.

Before reading my response to the phrase, continue to reflect on your understanding of "silence is violence" below. Consider including the following: [1] how you first heard the phrase, [2] how you currently understand it, and [3] how your racial identity forms how you understand it.

South African Archbishop Desmond Tutu made it explicit when he said: "If you are neutral in situations of injustice, you have chosen the side of the oppressor."[10]

In other words, there is no neutral ground with injustice. Our actions, speech, decisions, and values will either proliferate injustice or fight for justice; there is no space for neutrality. Indeed, attempting to stay neutral only reinforces the injustice already in place and provides fertile ground for it to continue and grow. The non-act of taking no side, Archbishop Tutu implores, in fact takes the side of the injustice.

In general, when the phrase *silence is violence* is used in anti-racism work, it is meant to compel people to speak against the status quo that upholds racism. In other words, the momentum behind the system and expressions of racism in place is so great that silence not only protects it but entrenches it. Staying silent in the face of racism, the phrase argues, neither reduces the violence of racism nor reduces our complicity in it. Rather, the act of staying silent is an act of violence itself, for which we must be accountable.

More specifically, "silence is violence" in anti-racism work is a charge rightfully aimed at those of us who are white. Naming our silence as violence exposes the lies we tell ourselves and others that our silence does nothing

---

[10]Desmond Tutu, *Oxford Essential Quotations*, 5th ed. (Oxford University Press, online version 2017), https://www.oxfordreference.com/view/10.1093/acref. The full quote attributed to Archbishop Desmond Tutu reads thus: "If you are neutral in situations of injustice, you have chosen the side of the oppressor. If an elephant has its foot on the tail of a mouse and you say that you are neutral, the mouse will not appreciate your neutrality."

or is neutral. When white people remain silent in the face of racism in any of its expressions, we are agreeing with racism and deeming it acceptable. Our proclamations that we disagree with specific racist words, policies, or practices, even that we don't believe they are true, are irrelevant. The consequences of white people's silence in response to racism is never anti-racist and is always concretely violent. Moreover, the violence we do with our silence is multifold.

- **The violence of the original racism:** Our silence becomes an expression of the original racism and thus participates in the original violence.

- **The violence of betrayal of our identity:** Our silence does violence to any claims of being anti-racist, including but not limited to discrediting our promises to fight against racism, exposing our hesitancy to contradict the lies of racism, and highlighting our unwillingness to risk the benefits we receive from racism.

- **The violence of betrayal of BIPAL people:** Our silence alerts BIPAL people to our allegiances to the benefits and protections of racism over their well-being, success, health, and survival (and thus, what should be grotesquely evident, any form of friendship or allyship).

- **The violence of the compounding consequences of racism as a system:** Because the consequences of racism cannot be limited to a one-time cause and effect, our silence generates more and more racism and the violence associated with it.

REFLECTIVE INTERNAL INTERROGATION

WRITE YOUR RESPONSE: How have you experienced or participated in the violence of white silence? Don't forget to think through the lens of your own racial identity.

Examples of white silence in the face of racism are increasingly plentiful. Let's consider two of them here: the business meeting, and "thoughts and prayers."

"Silence is Violence" in the Business Meeting

In addition to white people allowing racist remarks, stereotypes, and biases to remain unchallenged during meetings, those of us who are white do violence every time we steal the credit for an idea or solution offered by a BIPAL person. Meetings birthed and drenched in the templates of white supremacy, often invisible to those of us who are white, protect decision-makers and influencers who bypass, minimalize, and ignore ideas and solutions offered by BIPAL people, only to marvel at and celebrate the very same words later offered by a white person. When white people refuse to challenge this practice and explicitly or implicitly receive this credit, we are stealing the intellectual and productive labor of BIPAL people. The white people who argue vigilantly about properly cited sources and punishment for plagiarism are some of the same people who will not recognize the violence of white silence that unjustly credits white people with the creative and concrete labor of BIPAL people. Although BIPAL people have a multitude of reasons for staying silent in the face of racism in white-dominant spaces and meetings, those of us who are white must always speak out unless specifically told by a BIPAL person to remain silent.

The Violence of Silence in "Thoughts and Prayers"

Violent silence can also be cloaked in "good sounding words" or language that signifies nothing. The phrase "thoughts and prayers" in the wake of racialized terror events often does both.[11]

BIPAL people offer "thoughts and prayers" after racialized terror for multiple reasons, which span from anti-racism to internalized oppression. In these cases, "thoughts and prayers" might be an act of resistance or a way to focus their attention on centering the work and power of BIPAL people who intervene in times of deeply entrenched systemic oppression. However, at times, gatherings or statements of "thoughts and prayers" reflect assimilation to a white-dominant organization or a form of internalized oppression that prioritizes the comfort over the accountability of white people.

---

[11]As a white person, I always understand things through the lens of being white, even as I attempt to do the work of anti-racism. In my work as an anti-racism trainer, I work with and conduct workshops for both white and BIPAL people. I also have the privilege of working alongside the AME Church, a historically and unapologetically Black Christian denomination. These experiences of my own, and those that BIPAL people have shared with me, inform how I understand the strategies and reasoning behind the "thoughts and prayers" response to racialized terror events, as well as how I understand anti-racism work generally.

REAL TALK, though: For those of us who are white, every expression of "thoughts and prayers" that excludes very specific action-oriented anti-racist strategies is racist, and thus violent. Although thoughts and prayers literally say something, they are white silence because they do not *do* the work of anti-racism that concretely makes a change. The words are often used as placeholders signifying that the white person who speaks them knows nothing specific to say or enact to actually interrupt and dismantle racism.

Because we do not experience the harmful, even fatal consequences of racism, our words without tangible change reflect our lack of understanding and empathy for the depth of the pain and trauma effected by such events. Because of white segregation, the phrase "thoughts and prayers" reveals our unwillingness to avail ourselves of the abundant information about the realities of racism. Using this phrase also demonstrates unwillingness to find responses that don't trivialize the depth of the harm it (and other superficial responses) perpetrates. Finally, but not exhaustively, when those of us who are white respond to racial terror and trauma with our "thoughts and prayers," we center our own comfort level and timeline for creating and protecting REAL racial justice and equity.

For those of us who are white who commit to do anti-racism work, we must in all places and at all times override our lifelong training to protect our stake in the system of racism by staying silent. We must interrogate, not simply reflect upon, the ways in which our silence has been protective cover for our commitments to racism over and above the well-being, safety, survival, health, and thriving of Black, Indigenous, Pacific Islander, Asian, and Latino/x people. We must take stock of how our silence has perpetrated the same, different, and intensifying violence against people with whom we have dishonestly proclaimed our friendship, partnership, and alliance.

Yes, I said dishonestly—REAL TALK. Below, write your response to the way I have connected white people staying silent with dishonestly proclaiming our friendship, partnership, or alliance with BIPAL people. Name how your racial identity influences your answer.

REAL TALK means those of us who are white must never give ourselves permission to look away from the violent realities of our silence. Nor can we be allowed to ignore the stark language that exposes our deep commitment to allowing the system of racism to continue to benefit us over our proclamations of anti-racist intentions. REAL TALK means those of us who are white must continue anti-racism work with an equal and dual focus: on internal work that purges our diabolical commitment to benefit at the expense of BIPAL people and on external work that interrupts racism in every single expression.

Here's the thing: Every single anti-racism strategy, even something as central as "silence as violence," can be and is co-opted by white people to perpetrate and protect our racism. Thus, the disrupting and dismantling of racism must attend simultaneously to the violence of racism, the violence of silence—especially that of white silence—and the violence of racism that emerges from racist mimicry of anti-racism strategies themselves. Those of us who are white must refuse to stay silent, yes, but we must also refuse to attempt to coerce even anti-racist sounding words to protect our racism and erase our responsibility for it.

ACTION-NOW Learning Engagement: The Horizon of Silence

The Horizon of Silence

Righteous Silence	Silence of Learning	Protective Silence	Thoughts & Prayers	Silence Language	Repressive Silence
Holds space and time for the deep work of grief and truth-telling	Silence for learning anti-racism and unlearning racism	Protects oneself from the risks of racism or responsibilities of anti-racism	Empty phrases and inactive platitudes that perpetrate racism	Omission of words, phrases, and language	Overtalking that insists white voices, values, and standards are litmus tests for normalcy

This chapter has focused on REAL TALK and how "silence is violence" is used as an anti-racism strategy and simultaneously co-opted to perpetrate racism. This ACTION-NOW Learning Engagement utilizes what we're calling the Horizon of Silence to help identify how we can engage in REAL TALK. The diagram reflects a range of expressions of silence, from that which promotes anti-racism to that which protects racism. Each includes a brief description, an example, and several racially positioned action items you can use right now. Remembering that anti-racism work requires concrete actions that disrupt, dislodge, and dismantle racism, make your own commitment schedule to enact these REAL STRATEGIES in REAL TIME for REAL CHANGE.

RIGHTEOUS SILENCE

Description: The silence that holds space and time for the deep work of grief, discernment, and truth-telling. The enactment of holding silence for the work of anti-racism to occur. Here, the term, "righteous" is not limited to definitions related to faith. Rather, "righteous silence" refers to the deepest honoring of a person's wholeness.

Example: Holding "righteous silence" literally and figuratively creates spaces for BIPAL people to share their experiences of harm.

A BIPAL person shares their experiences of harm as a direct target of racism. Others, including BIPAL and white people, protect the space by keeping silent and refusing the temptation to interrupt silence, even with encouragement or meditations.

ACTION-NOW Learning Engagements:

For Black, Indigenous, Pacific Islander, Asian, and Latino/x people:

- Implement an act of resistance when someone else interrupts righteous silence. Be direct in expressing the need for centering BIPAL people to express our lament and grief in the aftermath of racialized terror. For example, call it out by saying to white people, "Practice decentering yourself by remaining silent," OR by saying to yourself or other BIPAL people, "We have a right to center our needs and to lament our grief in righteous silence."

For white people:

- Refuse to replace concrete anti-racism actions with "thoughts and prayers" statements or demonstrative gatherings. Research responsible ways to respond to racialized terror and trauma as directed by BIPAL authors and activists. Pay for learning by supporting artists and activists through Patreon (or through other platforms that support them), purchasing published works, or hiring BIPAL speakers and trainers.

For anyone:

- Practice resisting the urge to interrupt grief or testimonials with calls for reconciliation or inclusion declarations. Make note of specific times when you are most tempted to interrupt righteous silence. Name at least one phrase you will say to yourself to remind you of the importance of holding righteous silence.

SILENCE OF LEARNING

Description: The silence necessary for the learning of new information and anti-racism strategies and for the unlearning of the logic and expressions of racism.

Example: White people listening more to learn how to recognize racism in REAL TIME faster.

White people who are becoming more aware of the prevalence of racism, but who are still asking questions about specific examples or how to respond, should speak less and listen more.

ACTION-NOW Learning Engagements:

For Black, Indigenous, Pacific Islander, Asian, and Latino/x people:

- Believe other BIPAL people when they express their experiences of racism. Interrogate our responses to ensure they are not expressing ideologies and stereotypes stemming from internalized racism. Research and practice collaboration models of anti-racism among BIPAL people instead of using zero-sum models that reinforce racism and have BIPAL people fighting against each other. (See description of "Zero-Sum" models on page 63).

For white people:

- Believe Black, Indigenous, Pacific Islander, Asian, and Latino/x people when they express their experiences of racism and enact strategies they create or cosign as effective and meaningful. Interrogate any initial, even brief, responses of disbelief of BIPAL people's testimonials. Include also critical assessment of any of our immediate statements to defend our anti-racism including, "Oh, but I do believe BIPAL people."

- Name specifically how the anti-racism work you are doing right now has been *directly* influenced by or directed by a BIPAL testimonial or strategy. Practice doing that.

For anyone:

- Remember that we all have something more to learn. Practice paying attention to times when we need most to learn in silence. Take our racial positionality seriously by refusing to enact learning silence to shrink ourselves for white comfort (this is for BIPAL people), or to reenact the white supremacy that overvalues white people's wisdom and logic (this is for white people).

PROTECTIVE SILENCE

Description: The silence that protects oneself from risks of racism or the responsibilities of anti-racism.

Example: White people remain silent to protect themselves from losing status, reputation, position, or benefits.

A white person who has attended anti-racism workshops outlining scripted interruptions of racism allows a racist comment to occur in a meeting by their boss because they are afraid of losing their job and/or social status.

ACTION-NOW Learning Engagements:

For Black, Indigenous, Pacific Islander, Asian, and Latino/x people:

- Here, protective silence is a little different. The same strategies enacted by white people that perpetrate racism can sometimes be used by us to enact anti-racism. The focus is on our survival. For example, we might remain silent when our rights are being violated by a police officer to at least give ourselves a chance to survive the encounter.

For white people:

- Learn and practice scripts for interrupting racism in REAL TIME rather than relying on BIPAL people to do so. For example, when a white person interrupts a BIPAL person, look at the white person and say, "Excuse me." Then, look at the BIPAL person and ask, "Would you like to continue?" or "Did you have more to say?"

THOUGHTS AND PRAYERS

Description: The silence that reduces responses to empty phrases and inactive platitudes that perpetrate racism with more talk instead of encouraging the REAL TALK of anti-racism.

Example: A popular leader offers their thoughts and prayers on a Facebook post after the latest police-enacted racialized murder.

A popular mayor who reaches a wide audience of BIPAL and white people posts the following: "Offering our thoughts and prayers to the families of both the police officer and the victim during these trying times."

ACTION-NOW Learning Engagements:

For Black, Indigenous, Pacific Islander, Asian, and Latino/x people:

- Stop submitting to the guilt of being the only groups required to offer grace when justice is denied. Refuse to reduce acts of anti-racist resistance to words that remove our responsibility to be agents of REAL CHANGE in REAL TIME.

For white people:

- Never use the phrase "thoughts and prayers" as a response to racialized terror, because the phrase holds no anti-racism weight. Instead, call out the racism directly and stand with the BIPAL people directly impacted by following their lead and obeying their anti-racism strategies. REAL TALK: Interrogate any resistance you have to the phrase "obeying their anti-racism strategies."

For anyone:

- Refuse to create false equivalencies between the victim(s) and perpetrator(s) of racialized terror. Name specifically the responsibilities of the perpetrator to be accountable for their racism. Interrogate your need for more proof regarding who the true perpetrator is and the racism that upholds that need. Refuse any "both sides" arguments.

SILENCE LANGUAGE

Description: The silence assumed and enforced by the omission of words, phrases, and language that will change policies, practices, and standards from racist to anti-racist.

Example: A promotion board uses the word *effective* to evaluate managerial candidates' potential.

Although all evaluation committees have criteria for selection and training, when words like *effective, transformative leader*, and *culture fit* are used without specific definitions, all the racialized implicit bias, stereotypes, and prejudices present in the evaluation and evaluators are embedded within the evaluation standards that emerge from them.

ACTION-NOW Learning Engagements:

For Black, Indigenous, Pacific Islander, Asian, and Latino/x people:

- Review all legal, procedural, and best practices language and policies.

- Identify the language that silences and omits the factors of systemic racism that create and sustain racial inequities.

- Remember and internalize the words of Ms. Audre Lorde, who shared her daughter's Sankofa wisdom that "you're never really a whole person if you remain silent, because there's always that one little piece inside you that wants to be spoken out, and if you keep ignoring it, it gets madder and madder and hotter and hotter, and if you don't speak it out, one day it will just up and punch you in the mouth from the inside."[12]

- Create language that exposes the specific ways in which underlying systemic racism negatively and unequally burdens and harms BIPAL people and organizations.

For white people:

- Unlearn the word *share* when redistributing money from white organizations that have more capital and resources than BIPAL organizations. Remember the phrase "You can't share what you steal," and practice teaching other white people the specifics of how white supremacy and racism created an overabundance in white organizations to the detriment of BIPAL-led organizations.

---

[12]Audre Lorde, "The Transformation of Silence into Language and Action," in *Sister Outsider: Essays & Speeches by Audre Lorde* (Berkeley: Crossing Press, 2007), 42.

- Begin immediately using the term and enforcing the policies of *racial equity* instead of racial equality. Equality cannot be reached using measures of equality—adding the same amount to unequal starting points continues inequality. Equity recognizes and confronts historic, present, and compounding inequality, and it tries with concrete measures to address it.

For anyone: (for example, BMCR's open letter, 2020)[13]

- Look for and challenge all language (workplace, socio-political, legal, and so on) that prioritizes order instead of racial justice.

- Refuse to be distracted by strategy conversations that focus on the symptoms of racism instead of the structural racism that undergirds them.

- Unlearn the word *forgive* for debt incurred based in white supremacist policies and practices. Learn to use the word *reparations* to expose racialized inequities that have caused economic harm and that need to be redressed by concrete economic redistribution.

---

[13]While this document emerges from a church context, it focuses on institutionalized racist practices that also occur within businesses, schools, government, etc. Sheila M. Beckford, Tiffany French-Goffe, Dr. Richard Hayes, Dorlimar Lebron Malavé and Dr. Laurel Scott, "Open Letter to Bishop Bickerton," Black Methodists for Church Renewal NYAC, Google form, published July 30, 2020, https://docs.google.com/forms/d/e/1FAIpQLSflQML5 L95LWs3zw5m2CRSSfqxPJKkIINSPQ1bbQWaGSwjyLQ/viewform.

REPRESSIVE SILENCE

Description: The silence that restricts the ideologies, voices, and REAL anti-racism STRATEGIES of BIPAL people to uphold white supremacy. In layman's terms: overtalking that insists that white voices, values, and standards are the litmus test for normalcy.

Example: An organization (even a social justice organization) uses BIPAL "diversity hires" without organizational change.

An organization's hiring process includes a nondiscrimination statement, it boasts of a diversity and inclusion coordinator, and 5 percent of its workforce are employees of color, including one middle manager. The grooming policy in the HR handbook states that "hair should be clean, combed, and neatly trimmed or arranged."

ACTION-NOW Learning Engagements:

For Black, Indigenous, Pacific Islander, Asian, and Latino/x people:

- Challenge policies that pressure BIPAL people to conform to and internalize beauty standards of whiteness that uphold racism. For example, respond to discriminatory grooming policies by referencing the CROWN Act (or the Creating a Respectful and Open World for Natural Hair Act of 2020) passed initially in California, New York, New Jersey, and Virginia, and since passed in fourteen additional states, ten municipalities and the U.S. House of Representatives, which "prevents employers from creating and enforcing grooming policies that they say are race-neutral but really affect protected classes negatively and unequally."[14]

For white people:

- Name at least four ways the description of the company example above indicates policies or language that upholds white supremacy and racism. Do additional research if necessary, ensuring that you are listening to BIPAL voices.

---

[14]"Hair and Grooming Discrimination," WorkplaceFairness.org, accessed January 1, 2021, and https://www.jdsupra.com/legalnews/two-more-states-inact-crown-act-laws-3364285/, accessed August 31, 2022.

- Require your organization to hire an external BIPAL-owned company to complete a racial equity audit for all policies, practices, and procedures. Be unflinchingly willing to use and risk positional and social capital to do so.

For anyone:

- Work to create an anti-racist environment by naming and changing any policy or best practices list that demands repressive silence.
- Disrupt white overtalking.

Chapter 3:

REAL STRATEGIES

> REAL STRATEGIES prioritize ACTION-NOW Learning Engagements to move everyone beyond just talking about racism to immediate anti-racism actions. ACTION-NOW Learning Engagements are exercises that bridge the gap between learning about something and doing something. Rather than relying on models that demand that talk (REAL or otherwise) occur first and in isolation from action, REAL STRATEGIES place action at the center of Anti-Racism 4REALS. If anti-racism is anything that *actually* interrupts and dismantles racism, it just makes sense that actions are necessary. However, so much of current anti-racism practice is predicated on talking about and agreeing on truth of content, strategies necessary, and actions in order to engage. REAL STRATEGIES break the chains of information-only workshops—even at the introductory entry point—by creating processes by which action can be taken right now to dislodge, disrupt, and dismantle racism. Without real strategies, even the realest of REAL TALK becomes just more talk. REAL STRATEGIES make REAL TALK real.

LEDDER'S RESPONSE: During my time as an anti-racism trainer, I've come to realize that workshop hoarding is a real thing. Among those of us who are white, *gathering knowledge about* racism can actually become a substitute for *doing the work of* anti-racism. After racialized terror events, white organizations—including churches and social justice nonprofits—flood the emails and call logs of anti-racism groups begging* to schedule training sessions on white privilege, anti-racism, or implicit bias. With newly amplified shame or guilt or awareness, white people engage in a form of educational pornography—taking what we desire (information) without any of the responsibility for the work it takes to develop anything substantive (anti-racism change).

* Begging

REAL TALK: In literal and symbolic ways, white people and white-dominant organizations demand anti-racism training, especially after a racialized terror event. For example, after the murder of Mr. George Floyd in 2020, I received emails with attached speeches from white department managers telling me to correct their wording for anti-racism with their timeline attached. Some white leaders with HR or DEI responsibilities would provide one date (with a short timeline) for when they wanted to schedule a workshop while reminding me to adjust my content and tone to ensure that their white constituents would feel "invited into the work." Even in their heightened awareness of the need to do anti-racism work, the way they reached out for "help" to dismantle racism reinforced the white entitlement taught to us by white supremacy. More disturbing were the disgusting displays of entitlement spewed at BIPAL people doing this work. Patronizing, whitesplaining, coercing language that expected BIPAL people—especially Black women—to bend to white leaders' wishes, superficially coded in "we need to learn more." No mention of or space provided for them to process racialized terror events. Rather, even the most "progressive" of white leaders swiftly created false equivalencies between BIPAL people's pain and the need for those of us who are white to gain awareness and do the work of anti-racism. "Begging?" Nope. Straight-up racism without a shred of shame or humanity.

4REALS uses REAL STRATEGIES to get people into the work of anti-racism with the least amount of cushion and the fewest excuses to get out of it. Even the name of the exercises we use, ACTION-NOW Learning Engagements, has been crafted to highlight the urgency of the work and the immediacy of options.

In a very real way, REAL STRATEGIES provide entry points for every single person to have REAL options for doing the work of anti-racism as soon as they read the chapter, leave the workshop, or click "leave meeting." By using entry points instead of journey language, we eliminate all concern or any excuses that not all people are ready to do the work of anti-racism right now. This doesn't mean in any way, however, that some people will still not do the work of anti-racism. But that is a choice that REAL STRATEGIES brings to the surface. The reality that every single white person can do anti-racism work right now presents an opportunity for rationalizations against us doing so to rise to the surface for assessment and critique. Words like "Well, I would, but . . ." or "I don't understand how . . ." or any of the plethora of excuses those of us who are white have been allowed to get away with, hold no weight when options for the immediate are presented. For those of us who are white, our anti-racism work must necessarily dislodge, disrupt, and dismantle all excuses for not doing whatever it takes to eradicate racism in all of its forms every single time it shows up.

INTERNAL ASSESSMENT: Write here your first thoughts after reading the sentence below.

> *For those of us who are white,*
> ***every single one of our excuses***
> *for not doing the work of anti-racism*
> *right now **is racist**.*

One way REAL STRATEGIES help to do the work of anti-racism is by removing the justifications racism has taught us to use to delay or refuse to do the work. Some of these justifications include saying that it's okay for us to wait, that we need to do more research first, or that we need to be "ready" to get started. These excuses show up and cross over our individual, interpersonal, and work lives.

(Not Even Close to the Full List of) Excuses White People Use to Avoid Doing Anti-Racism Work Now

White people: *Check off all the excuses you have used and write below each check mark what action you will take the next time this excuse comes up for you.*

BIPAL people: *Check all excuses you have heard white people use and write below each check mark what action you will take (or not take) the next time this excuse comes up in front of you.*

❑ The rate of loans/my history with my bank/the complicated nature of accounts with my bank is such that transferring my money/accounts/loans/mortgage to a Black-owned bank wouldn't be "smart" at this time.

❑ You have to understand, my family is just "that way." They don't know any better; they grew up in a different time; they don't mean anything by it; they're stuck in their ways; this is my family/heritage/blood; or they're going to take time to change.

❑ I'm just one person in a huge or complex organization (business, nonprofit, government agency, university, society, corporation)—nothing I do will make a difference.

❑ I have to hold on to my character and values even as I do anti-racism work, so I will not sacrifice being polite/civil/courteous/nice/good when confronting racism or people.

❑ I agree with the message but not the tactics.

This exercise serves (at least) a dual purpose. First, it provides a list of common excuses (and types of excuses) used to get out of doing anti-racism work by those of us who are white. When white people see this list, it not only challenges us to name specifically the excuses we use, it also makes our brains acutely aware of when they show up in the future. You know how after you buy a red car you all of a sudden see a bunch of red cars on the road? It's not because there was a boom in red car sales. It's because your brain has been primed to see them. Same thing here.[15]

Second, the exercise confronts those of us who are white with the specific task of determining ahead of time what we will do instead. Here, we may have already learned from our reading, from workshops, or from BIPAL people directly what actions are necessary to counter our racism. However, often we have ignored the vast knowledge available, and discredited the BIPAL people who write, share, and present it, because of the way white segregation and white supremacy work, respectively. Thus, at this point it may be necessary to do the work required to learn what to do and how to do it. This is part of our work as white people—and we can't disrupt, dislodge, and dismantle racism without it.

---

[15]E. Michelle Ledder first used this example when writing a workbook called *Implicit Bias: What We Don't Think We Think* during her time at the General Commission on Religion and Race (GCORR).

Ledder's REAL TALK: Just because I write about anti-racism and deeply believe that those of us who are white must enact anti-racism strategies without excuse, that doesn't mean there is any way I can get from my own whiteness to anti-racism work without intervention. In other words, I have had to learn directly and indirectly from BIPAL people what strategies are needed to disrupt, dislodge, and dismantle racism. I didn't wake up one day and figure out anti-racism. It is impossible for me, as a white person, to create out of nothing any of these strategies without first learning the strategies BIPAL people have created. Additionally, even after learning about REAL STRATEGIES, the reality is that I don't always implement them at all, implement them correctly, or implement them without sweat rolling down my back as I do. White supremacy has taught me to protect my unearned racialized privileges and benefits by keeping quiet, by staying out of it, and by ignoring my responsibility to dismantle racism wherever and whenever it shows up. I must commit without reserve to do this work no matter how I feel or how I fail. REAL STRATEGIES don't become REAL without implementation—and implementation only becomes REAL with accountability (more in the REAL CHANGE chapter).

It might seem as if this is the perfect segue into anti-racism to-do and not-to-do lists. And please believe that they are coming. However, we'll first pull back the pedagogical veil to reveal the art and science of anti-racism teaching. By looking at anti-racism to-do and not-to-do lists *as a strategy* (before looking at what they actually say to do or not to do), those of us who are white can be better prepared to avoid the racism we enact when we do the "right thing" in the wrong way. By considering how to-do and not-to-do anti-racism lists are constructed, white people can reduce the racism we perpetrate through appropriation, white saviorism, and white supremacy.

Anti-racism to-do and not-to-do lists are a strategy in and of themselves. I want to be clear—I am not damning to-do and not-to-do lists. They're a great place to start when people are just learning about a subject or just beginning the actions of putting learning into place. When created and followed honorably, anti-racism to-do and not-to-do lists can bring the "more talk" pseudo-anti-racism into the work of dislodging, disrupting, and dismantling racism. When asked by white people where to start—or when white people say they don't know where to start—I often tell them to do a critical Google search for "ten things we wish white allies would do" and "ten things we wish white allies would stop doing" lists written by BIPAL people—and for such a time as this, by Black people specifically.

What this *does not mean*, though, is that white people can begin critiquing these lists or the BIPAL people who wrote them. Rather, when those of us who are white first start out, we have little to no experience with discerning whether a particular strategy is honorable for us to engage in. Thus, a critical search in this context means to find three to five lists in each category (again, written by BIPAL people generally, and right now Black people specifically) and look for the overlap. Then start doing those things. BIPAL people do not think, act, live, write, suggest, protest, resist, invite, struggle, demand, challenge, strategize, or anything else as a monolith. It is impossible to find one anti-racism to-do or not-to-do list that will encapsulate everything BIPAL people advise white people to do or not do to fight against racism. However, by starting with the overlap, those of us who are white can be primed to do the least amount of damage and perpetrate the least amount of racism while following the to-do or not-to-do anti-racism lists.

Did it shock you that I said "least amount of damage and racism" instead of "the greatest amount of good?" Why or why not? How does this refine your anti-racism work? **WRITE YOUR RESPONSES HERE**

Having a starting point or even a finely curated anti-racism to-do or not-to-do list doesn't eliminate the possibility that those of us who are white will perpetrate racism while using them. Here, it is most likely that white people who identify ourselves as liberal or progressive will use these lists in ways that enact the expressions of racism for which we are most known. There are many entry points for dismantling these expressions of ally-list racism, but one to start with is the one from the 4REALS introduction: racial positionality.

Racial positionality says that because we live in a racialized society, and because society has different rules, treatment, benefits, protections, and punishments depending on our racial identities, we experience the world—and the world experiences us—differently based on race. When we start hearing "We all have different work to do" regarding anti-racism, this is where that starts. We have different risks, responsibilities, and work because of where we are positioned within the system of racism. White people have been shoving our work onto the backs of BIPAL people this whole time, which is why the system and its expressions still exist and why BIPAL people have been fighting and resisting it their whole lives. Because BIPAL people are the direct targets of racism, they are the most capable of determining strategies or lists with anti-racist outcomes and which kinds of work white people should implement.

> *Interrupting white people's racism is*
> *always the work of white people.*
> *No matter what BIPAL people decide*
> *are their strategies, we remain steadfast*
> *knowing it is always part of our work,*
> *no matter what.*

Even within the same category of anti-racism work, the work of white people and the work of BIPAL people are often different. Addressing and dealing with white manipulation (fragility) is a perfect example with which we should start. *White fragility* is a term often used in anti-racism work and heard more frequently since white sociologist Robin DiAngelo got the term published in her book of the same name. Although it is a phenomenon recognized and resisted by BIPAL people for as long as racism has existed, DiAngelo often receives unmitigated citation credit misinformed by white privilege and supremacy. A paraphrase of the published term's definition describes the symbolic but very real line, in conversations about racism or work to dismantle it, that when crossed makes white people so uncomfortable that we engage in a set of predictable acts or reactions, including but not limited to pouting, silence, shutting down, crying, anger, defense, and walking out.

When groups that include white people ask for anti-racism training and have a needs list that rivals the eternal length of pi, or the limit that they can only "do one training for now," I usually recommend a workshop on white manipulation (fragility). When white people are involved, whether we are dominant in numbers or entitlement, white manipulation (fragility) will obstruct even the best anti-racism strategies. White manipulation (fragility) is the weaponization of whiteness and of humanness for the sake of whiteness. Left unchecked, it creates a power vortex that sucks up all the attention and energy that should be focused on race, racism, and anti-racism and coerces it to care for and protect white people. Emotions and responses of discomfort are not bad in and of themselves. However, when these are used as weapons to manipulate energy and people in order to coddle the very ones responsible for the racism, they are racist.

And here's where racial positionality comes back into play. It's not just that white people enact white manipulation (fragility) and thus are responsible for it—though we do and we are. It's that to dismantle white manipulation (fragility), we must engage in different strategies based on our racial identity. White people must build our *resilience* to white manipulation (fragility). Those of us who are white must resist the temptation to weaponize our emotions, reactions, and whiteness to get away with our racism and away from our responsibility for it. To do so, we build up our *resilience* to the reactionary responses we have relied upon to alleviate our guilt and shame. All resilience against our white manipulation (fragility) is built for the purpose of doing more and more anti-racism work before our white manipulation (fragility) kicks up again. White people must, at all times, refuse to demand care from BIPAL people or minimize our responsibility for our own racism and white manipulation (fragility). We must work to dislodge, disrupt, and dismantle our racism without putting that burden on our BIPAL counterparts.

BECKFORD'S RESPONSE: Just recently I purchased a set of fabric resistance bands for strengthening purposes. I underwent a procedure some years ago that left me with a limited range of motion. I first used bands made of rubber to achieve the same purpose; however, the rubber bands rolled up and I would have to pause my workout to fix them. After learning about the fabric resistance bands, I did my reading, then made a purchase.

I used the first-level fabric band for a few days. It was a bit of a struggle until I got into a groove. I found that as I continued to use the band, my routine became easier, even though as I stretched the band, the resistance increased. I used the first-level band for a time before realizing that the band had done its job. I had achieved a level of strength, but I could not progress if I continued using the same level. I moved up to the next level of resistance represented by a different color. I began with pink, then moved to gray as my leg muscles *were conditioned* to the first level of resistance.

BIPAL people have been taught via "the talk," oral stories, historical facts, and our present reality through racialized terror to be resilient, but resistance is something we must build up. Philip Spencer Lake's comparison between resilience and resistance is helpful here: "The capacity to weather a disturbance without loss is defined as resistance, whereas resilience is the capacity to recover from a disturbance after incurring losses." In other words, resilience requires loss, while resistance prevents loss.[16]

We, BIPAL people, have got to do better in building resistance to white supremacy and racism. Knowing the stories and conjuring up the resistance our ancestors had will help. Since the killing of Mr. George Floyd, I have noticed many of our people posting the most disrespectful meme that dishonors the strength, tenacity, resilience, resistance, and "stick-to-itiveness" of our ancestors.

This meme replicates the lies of the whitewashed history retold by conditioned BIPAL people that our ancestors were not the authors of change but simply submissive to the whims and wills of white people. Yet, it is only because of their determination to resist dehumanization that we are even here to continue the demands for respect, liberation, justice, equity and the command to "keep your knee off of our necks!"

- Whitewashed history will make you think the Rev. Dr. Martin Luther King Jr. was the most beloved "Negro" at the time of his life and death, but research tells us that he had a 75 percent disapproval rating in 1968.[17]

- Whitewashed history will make you believe that Rosa Parks refused to give up her seat because the Civil Rights Movement was a movement for all people, as taught to my child by her white elementary school teacher.

---

[16]Philip S. Lake, "Resistance, Resilience and Restoration," *Ecological Management & Restoration* 14, no. 1, (2012): 20, https://doi.org/10.1111/emr.12016.

[17]James C. Cobb, "Even Though He Is Revered Today, MLK Was Widely Disliked by the American Public When He Was Killed," *Smithsonian Magazine* (April 4, 2018), https://www. smithsonianmag.com/history/why-martin-luther-king-had-75-percent-disapproval-rating-year-he-died-180968664/.

- Whitewashed history will make you believe that the war on drugs was not a strategy to incarcerate BIPAL people, mainly Black and Latino/x people.[18]

- Whitewashed history told by conditioned BIPAL people would make you believe that slaves were immigrants.[19]

These fallacies of whitewashed history are not just history. Legacies of pulling yourself up by your bootstraps are repeated today without factoring in the long history of oppressive systems such as redlining, racially discriminatory hiring, white flight, the underfunding of educational institutions, and the overfunding of the prison industrial complex.

BIPAL people have become conditioned to accept and expect racism. Some of us continue to use the beginning level of resistance until our anti-racism muscles atrophy. As our muscles continue to weaken even as we mimic the movements of resistance, our best efforts can no longer disrupt, dislodge, and dismantle racism. We must be like our ancestors, whose strategies of resistance included the following:

- Not laziness but intentional "slowdowns"

- Not passive aggressiveness but premeditated and calculated action plans

- Not submission to white supremacy but tactical measures used to select leadership of their choosing

- Not non-threating BIPAL leadership that earned the approval of white people or a white system, but audacious leadership that defies and rejects whiteness as "truth" and normalcy

Internalized oppression turns BIPAL people against BIPAL people while we do the bidding of white supremacy.

---

[18]Michelle Alexander, *The New Jim Crow: Mass Incarceration in the Age of Colorblindness* (New York: New Press, 2010) pp. 120–122.

[19]Liam Stack, "Ben Carson Calls Slaves 'Immigrants' in First HUD Remarks," *The New York Times* (March 6, 2017), https://www.nytimes.com/2017/03/06/us/politics/ben-carson-refers-to-slaves-as-immigrants-in-first-remarks-to-hud-staff.html.

For BIPAL people only: Share a time when you either witnessed, participated in, or urged an action that perpetrated racialized harm against your BIPAL sibling. **White people, DO NOT RESPOND!**

_____

_____

_____

_____

_____

_____

_____

_____

For white people: Knowing that the previous question is off-limits to you, interrogate your reaction to the instruction "DO NOT RESPOND!"

_____

_____

_____

_____

_____

_____

_____

_____

Resistance to whiteness as normalcy is imperative to anti-racism work. BIPAL people must identify (interrogate) the lure of provocative means of advancement that forces us to denounce our thoughts, ideas, history, and ancestral teachings and accept whiteness—white thoughts, white value systems, white religion, and white mediocrity—as a measure of success. Resistance must decenter whiteness. One REAL STRATEGY to decenter whiteness calls for us to cease coddling white people's manipulation (fragility). White people's manipulation (fragility) is usually coded as a response to an attack on the white person. When white people use the term "attack" to describe being confronted with their racism, this is a tactic to take the focus off of the racism and recenter whiteness. It is also a signal for other white people to join in, and it elicits sympathy or coddling from BIPAL people. What I mean by coddling white manipulation (fragility) is coming to the white person's rescue, making the offending white person feel as if they are more important than the offended BIPAL person, and allowing white manipulation (fragility) to recenter whiteness when the concern should be focused on dislodging, disrupting, and dismantling racism.

For BIPAL people: How often have you witnessed or participated in coddling white people's manipulation (fragility)? Please check all that apply to you; then explain how these acts coddle white people.

- ❏ They don't know any better.
- ❏ They did not mean it that way.
- ❏ I know their heart.
- ❏ You are making this about race when they are hurting.
- ❏ Can we take a break?
- ❏ What they mean by this is . . .
- ❏ They are trying, give them credit.
- ❏ They didn't grow up around BIPAL people, so they don't know.
- ❏ We need to say it in a way that does not offend.
- ❏ They feel attacked.
- ❏ This doesn't bring unity.

For white people: How many of these have been used on your behalf or used specifically by you to protect your own white manipulation (fragility) or that of another white person? Please check all that apply. In the lines below, explain how these actually perpetrate racism.

- ❏ I feel attacked.
- ❏ I didn't know that was racist.
- ❏ I never had BIPAL friends growing up.
- ❏ I didn't mean that.
- ❏ I would never hurt anyone.
- ❏ My feelings are hurt
- ❏ (More tears)
- ❏ You don't understand.
- ❏ Why are you making this about race?/Not everything is about race.
- ❏ I'm not like them/those other white people. (Yes, this is white manipulation [fragility].)
- ❏ I've marched in many protests.
- ❏ I have a Black Lives Matter sign on my lawn.

The reality of white manipulation (fragility) is not new to BIPAL people. White tears, defending, deflecting, and making a conflict about hurt feelings is a strategy that white people use to distance themselves from the evils of their racism.

White people's manipulation (fragility) also influences who BIPAL people select to lead in our own communities. If a BIPAL person is too loud or too outspoken in our own communities, we determine that that particular person with those characteristics could not lead because "no one" (meaning white folk) will follow them. BIPAL leaders shun them, try to tell them to tone it down, or make disparaging remarks about them. In most cases, BIPAL people's primary goal is not to hinder each other's growth. This is not the crabs-in-a-barrel mentality that we often hear about. It is coddling whiteness to the detriment of our own advancement.

> *The crabs-in-a-barrel mentality:*
> *Crabs are thrown in a wooden barrel.*
> *As one advances to the top, another*
> *crab grabs its leg to attempt its own escape.*
> *However, the outcome prevents*
> *both crabs from getting out.*
> *I always ask: "Who made the barrel? What was*
> *its purpose? Who put the crabs in the barrel?"*

I recall having a loud disagreement with a man outside. An older Black woman approached me without knowing the events leading up to the argument and said, "A lady doesn't carry herself that way; Black women must be quiet but strong. That's how we survived [enslavement]." After returning home and sharing these events with my mother, she said, "Served him right! A lady knows how to be ready to defend herself." With that one statement, my mother shut some doors inside of me and opened another. From that day forward, hearing those words and the message of liberation that they instilled in me, I vowed to be my own definition of a lady and no one else's. That moment formed me and breathed into me a new understanding of the responsibility of resisting "respectability politics" and defying the effects of white supremacy no matter from whom they come.

> *We are trained to be*
> *what whiteness determines us to be.*
> *We are conditioned to accept leaders*
> *who will conform to whiteness.*
> *Anti-racist REAL STRATEGIES*
> *demand the opposite.*

White people understand racial positionality well. They have used it in their playbook to further their agenda to create structures that allow them to remain in power and to divide BIPAL people as a tactic. Plays found there begin with positioning BIPAL people in desirable places of authority to use us for optics. Once we're there, they pressure us to challenge anti-racist legislation that would provide for equity, accountability, transparency, and other means of resistance. Historically, white people then misuse the BIPAL people's positioning to weaken BIPAL structures of resistance in order to infiltrate, control, and manipulate outcomes in favor of strengthening white supremacy through effective racist policies and structures. BIPAL people, both wittingly and unwittingly, have been engaged in white supremacist tactics that further divide our communities.

Resistance as a REAL STRATEGY requires BIPAL people's refusal to play by any racist playbook—which first requires that we know it. Resistance for us will also include nonparticipation in any promotion, lure, or perk that results in strengthening white supremacy and dividing BIPAL communities. REAL STRATEGIES of resistance will also place a priority upon anti-racism audits of policies and procedures to ensure that all racist practices are eliminated. Risk is a factor in any means of resistance, but any action of freedom or resistance is risky. We must ask ourselves, what is the alternative?

ACTION-NOW Learning Engagement

Using racial positionality, follow the REAL STRATEGY listed for your racial identity to honorably and authentically do the work of anti-racism right now.

REAL STRATEGY	BIPAL People	White People	All People
Address white manipulation (fragility)	Commit to not coming to the rescue of white people when they are confronted with their own racism and their attempts to take attention away from their offense. **Call out white manipulation (fragility); do not coddle.**	Build resilience to our own white manipulation (fragility) through the following steps: [1] Learn to manage our emotions and refuse to allow them to demand the energy and attention that should be going toward the work of anti-racism; [2] refuse to expect BIPAL people to care for us while we deal with our own guilt, shame, and awareness of our racism; and [3] refuse to defend ourselves after learning of our racism ("I didn't mean …" or "I didn't know …"). Rather, take the time and give the effort necessary to learn why what we did is racist and what to do instead.	Refuse to allow white manipulation (fragility) to be acceptable.

ACTION-NOW Learning Engagement

Using racial positionality, follow the REAL STRATEGY listed for your racial identity to honorably and authentically do the work of anti-racism right now.

REAL STRATEGY	BIPAL People	White People	All People
Honor BIPAL-only spaces	BIPAL people reserve the option to invite or not to invite white people. There are few spaces where BIPAL people can be themselves without judgement or the expectation to follow norms created by white people. Remember racial positionality when thinking about allowing yourself to be in a space where you have the option to invite or not to invite.	Pay close and careful attention to directions and descriptions of gathering spaces to check whether this is a BIPAL-only space. Learn and look for wording (explicit) and coding (culturally specific language) that indicates a BIPAL-only space. Learn why BIPAL-only spaces are critical and how and why white people invading them perpetrates racism and white supremacy. When (and only when) invited into a BIPAL-only space by a BIPAL person, do not speak unless asked specifically, and be especially careful to obey instructions as to what they are asking for us to do.	Do not create false equivalencies between BIPAL-only spaces and white segregated spaces. Do not create BIPAL-only spaces as an afterthought or add-on, or in less-than-desirable/visible areas.

ACTION-NOW Learning Engagement

Using racial positionality, follow the REAL STRATEGY listed for your racial identity to honorably and authentically do the work of anti-racism right now.

REAL STRATEGY	BIPAL People	White People	All People
Rest	Anti-racism work is extremely taxing on the bodies, minds, and spirits of BIPAL people. We can burn out while doing anti-racism work because we can never turn off our racial identity. We can try to assimilate, play respectability politics, or define ourselves by nationality to be removed from the scrutiny, harm, and racism that white supremacy thrives on, but our skin color, accents, language and culture often give us away. White allies/accomplices can easily walk away from this work (rest). Because we are not a part of the social construction of whiteness, rest is an essential component of the resistance strategy we must create for ourselves.	A basic balance of rest and work is necessary for all human beings, but white people must also realize that feeling tired, worn out, and burned out from the work of anti-racism is part of our work. We must not create a false equivalency between our tiredness from doing work to repudiate harm that we've caused and the tiredness of BIPAL people who are experiencing harm and physical/psychological/emotional exhaustion as part of their experience as a BIPAL person. Consider the weariness we feel a glimpse of what BIPAL people experience and a continuous call to keep doing this work despite it.	Rest is a requirement for all human beings. Regular and balanced rest promotes the health necessary to continue to interrupt racism in REAL TIME. Burnout and self-adulatory martyrdom are not anti-racist.

ACTION-NOW Learning Engagement

Using racial positionality, follow the REAL STRATEGY listed for your racial identity to honorably and authentically do the work of anti-racism right now.

REAL STRATEGY	BIPAL People	White People	All People
BIPAL-created anti-racism strategies	Strategies that benefit BIPAL people should be created by those who are the direct targets of racism. Those who experience the harm of racism are those who know how to disrupt, dislodge, and dismantle it. Hold white allies/accomplices/people accountable for co-opting or plagiarizing the work of BIPAL people.	Follow the overarching template of anti-racism work: BIPAL people create or sign off on anti-racism strategies, white people implement the work and credit BIPAL people for it, and white people are accountable to BIPAL people for doing it correctly and responsibly. We do not appropriate the work or words or strategies of BIPAL people, recognizing that there is no pathway from our own whiteness to anti-racism work without an intervention of some sort.	Teach strategies based in racial positionality

ACTION-NOW Learning Engagement

Using racial positionality, follow the REAL STRATEGY listed for your racial identity to honorably and authentically do the work of anti-racism right now.

REAL STRATEGY	BIPAL People	White People	All People
Transfer money into institutions owned by BIPAL people	Transfer mortgages as well as business and personal accounts to Black-owned credit unions and banks. Buy Black. BIPAL people, protect your investments; invest in your communities; realize your economic power; and refuse to undervalue your worth. Place value—monetary or otherwise—on the anti-racism strategies we create and white people use.	Transfer all accounts, loans, mortgages, and credit card balances to BIPAL-owned institutions; use our social and leadership power in any organizations we are a part of to encourage others to transfer their accounts, loans, and mortgages to the same. Do not, however, transfer money into Black- or BIPAL-owned credit unions. The ownership of credit unions is determined by the accounts of the people, and thus, if enough white people transfer money into credit unions, we shift the ownership from BIPAL people to white people, furthering economic inequity.	Create economic racial equity

61

ACTION-NOW Learning Engagement

Using racial positionality, follow the REAL STRATEGY listed for your racial identity to honorably and authentically do the work of anti-racism right now.

REAL STRATEGY	BIPAL People	White People	All People
"Begging" / Asking for help in anti-racism work	**BIPAL PEOPLE ARE NOT OBLIGATED TO TEACH WHITE PEOPLE ABOUT RACISM.**	Interrogate whether our language (verbal or body) demands that BIPAL people help us with our anti-racism work because we've now decided it's important. Remember that it is our responsibility to obey the strategies created or cosigned by BIPAL people, but it is not their job to teach us, and even if they decide to do so, that is never on our timeline. Critically assess our language through the lens of someone who is harmed by the injustice we want to learn about. Would you recoil if an abuser asked the person they abused for "help" using the same language we use to "ask" BIPAL people for help in anti-racism work?	

ACTION-NOW Learning Engagement

Using racial positionality, follow the REAL STRATEGY listed for your racial identity to honorably and authentically do the work of anti-racism right now.

REAL STRATEGY	BIPAL People	White People	All People
Refuse to pit BIPAL people against BIPAL people	Refuse to accept the stereotype of the "crabs in a barrel" as our own reality. Resist buying into the white supremacy playbook. The playbook is to always act as if one group is speaking adversely about the other. In other words, an employer says they "would" make changes based on racial equity but can't because of competing demands from different groups of color (BIPAL people). This is a tactic used to plant seeds of discord and inevitably take the focus off of the main source of division: racism.	Learn and expose how white supremacy limits resources, access, opportunities, space, and respect for BIPAL people. Recognize how white supremacy often creates separate and unequal buckets for "everyone" and for BIPAL people—and how doing so siphons all BIPAL people to the smaller bucket to compete with each other while equating "everyone" with white people/groups. Take a look at how BIPAL people are only offered or told about money/scholarships specifically set apart for BIPAL people but not about the money/scholarships/grants for "everyone," even though they are eligible for both.	Dismantle the zero-sum game lie. White supremacy is based in the zero-sum game, which says that if one person or group has some, there is less for everyone else. White supremacy and racism are founded on a scarcity model that keeps people and groups in competition with each other for a limited amount of resources, including but not limited to money, jobs, excellence, and even benefit of the doubt. In contrast, anti-racism highlights how oppressions and injustices create scarcity and pit people against each other. White supremacy lies to us all that white people deserve (and deserve the most) resources and must exclude all others to protect themselves.

ACTION-NOW Learning Engagement

Using racial positionality, follow the REAL STRATEGY listed for your racial identity to honorably and authentically do the work of anti-racism right now.

REAL STRATEGY	BIPAL People	White People	
Decentering whiteness	Resist recentering whiteness. Resist defending white manipulation (fragility). Resist conforming to white supremacy.	Stop saying, immediately, that we will "give up our spot" for BIPAL peoples — this defines the position as ours to give up (or "share" — this is the same thing!) — rather say, "I am stepping down, my staying reinforces and centers whiteness."	
Honor BIPAL-selected leadership	BIPAL people elect, affirm, and empower their own leaders. BIPAL people do not use the master's tools to dismantle the master's house.[20] Leadership is not to be selected based on criteria created by whiteness.	Obey BIPAL-selected leadership decisions and the leaders they select. Interrogate your first (and second) reaction to the word obey. Assess the racism and white supremacy behind any resistance to BIPAL-selected leadership. Refuse to use the phrase "I agree with the goal but not the tactics."	

[20] Lorde, Sister *Outsider*, 112.

Chapter 4:

REAL TIME

> Racism happens in real time, so anti-racism must also happen in REAL TIME. REAL TIME incorporates role-playing so that people can practice scripts and rehearse plans in preparation to interrupt and dismantle racism in the moment.

REAL TALK and REAL STRATEGIES can't interrupt and dismantle racism if we can't enact them when the racism occurs. But REAL TIME also addresses how racism itself obstructs the urgent necessity and the required skill sets for interrupting it. Social currency, corporate climbing culture, and the zero-sum game are all methods that white supremacy uses to create boundaries—real and imagined—that teach us, based on our racial positionality, to obey the logic system of racism. This logic system is complete with rules and values and the ordering and timing of "proper" ways to do things. Anti-Racism 4REALS has seen how interrupting racism in REAL TIME subverts and dismantles racism because it belongs to the logic system of anti-racism.

A few notes before we get started:

- Remember, REAL TIME means that anti-racism starts before the reading, learning, or workshop ends. Even the way we learn about anti-racism can teach anti-racism.

- *Everyone* is ready to do anti-racism work. 4REALS deeply believes that to dismantle oppression is part of what it means to be ethical. Some people might not have the tools or resolve yet, but all people can do anti-racism work right now.

- 4REALS doesn't use journey language that tricks people into thinking the time to act comes later. Rather, we use entry points highlighting how everyone can do something as soon as they finish the chapter, leave the workshop, or click "leave meeting."

- *Anti-racism only re-enacts the interruption in role-playing scenarios.* When white people ask for the roleplay to include the racism so they can "recognize it," they reveal how much of their lives are steeped in white segregation, how they haven't bothered to do their own research, and how diminished their empathy must be to request a role-playing session of harm when it doesn't directly harm them.

LEDDER'S RESPONSE:

In the business world, the adage to "meet the people where they are" provides a strategic method for assessing employee needs. Rather than the employer deciding what the employee needs without consultation, employees are offered the opportunity to share what they need to perform their job well. More than another performance checklist, "meeting the people where they are" attempts to see the humanness of employees. This leadership style is often partnered with "you have to respect the people." Coupled together, these imperatives—"you have to respect the people" and "meet the people where they are"—are meant to create a workplace that values the well-being of its employees. Respectful interactions guide leaders to see where people are struggling—even failing—then address their needs compassionately to find a better way of working and learning alongside one another.

Imagining and hoping for employees, at any level, who "do business" with respect and utilize human-centered savvy, provides an oasis in a world hell-bent on critiquing employees (and executives) into submissive obedience. The promise of respect as a central value that corrects with compassion instead of coercing with chastisements is as alluring as it is addictive. Employee well-being and productivity, it is argued, can exist concomitantly with company/brand loyalty increasing all the while. Changes in the workplace have the potential to create changes in society. And perhaps, if this promise is left in the idealized state and outside of anti-racism work, the world would be a better place. So then, how could respect and meeting the people where they are be wrong?

In anti-racism work, it is clear to most that outcomes must override intentions. No matter how good the intentions are, if the outcomes create harm, there is no intention good enough to erase that harm. For example, let's say I'm presenting in a meeting at the front of the room and someone jumps up from their seat, runs across the room toward me, and stomps on my foot as they run past me out the door. In the immediacy of that event, we might all look around at each other wondering what in the world just happened. In addition, I am in searing pain and unable to stand or walk using my injured foot. Three minutes later, the runner reenters the room with an ice cream cone and explains that he had received a text saying that mocha-chip ice cream cones were being offered in the conference room, and he just couldn't get there fast enough. He says he didn't mean to step on my foot, but the lure of mocha-chip ice cream was just too powerful for him to take anything else into consideration. I immediately understand, since mocha-chip ice cream is clearly the most superior ice cream flavor of them all (prove me wrong ☺). However, this doesn't change the fact that I will need to go to the emergency room because the swelling in my foot is so bad that I won't be able to (nor should I have to) walk it off. Our relationship might be salvaged, because I understand his intention was not to harm me. But the harm has been done, must be addressed separately, and cannot be reversed with his explanation.

In anti-racism work with white people, the imperatives to "respect the people" and "meet the people where they are" are corrupted to satisfy our need to be right, to be protected from any type of shame or guilt, and to be cared for even in the midst of our racism. "Respect the people" is corrupted into an imperative to accept people's racist behaviors, beliefs, and values as if respect were the same thing as permission. When this happens, horrid behavior becomes equated with someone's opinion, someone's upbringing, or someone's personhood. In terms of white people and our racism, the first allows our "I" statements to protect racism, the second allows "heritage" to mask harm, and the third allows abuse to imitate empathy. But true (or REAL) respect doesn't permit oppression—it corrects it. Actual respect for another person wouldn't allow them to repeat or re-create harmful conditions—whether that harm is toward self or others. Rather, REAL respect—especially mutual respect—desires for each party to live into their best selves, inside and outside of the workplace. Respect doesn't bifurcate a person into what they do at work and who they are outside of it. While we pretend we can compartmentalize ourselves in this way, true respect "meets us where we ACTUALLY are" to remind us we cannot. Respect, then, in anti-racism work, will not shy away from whatever it takes to create the humane environments within which equity is free to be made manifest.

But what does this have to do with REAL TIME? Here's where it all comes together: By combining the false sense of respect with "meet the people where they are," white people are allowed to continue to perpetrate racism, until, on our own timeline, we decide we are *ready* to change. When "respect the people" equates to permission to continue perpetrating racism, "meet the people where they are" equates to a directive to wait *until* the people give their permission for change to occur. The main problem with this, though there are many, is that our ability to choose for ourselves what we do or not do (agency—a good thing) is conflated with our right to keep perpetrating racism (oppression). For those of us who are white, this combination is intoxicating in that it privileges our standing as "good" people, protects our affair with white supremacy, and permits our entitlement to do things on our own timeline. Although we are the ones who are committing harm, who are at fault, and who are benefiting from the oppression of BIPAL people, we demand to feel "safe" (read here, comfortable) in order to make changes. This deadly combination allows our racism in all its expressions to continue based on the timeline of the oppressor—us. In no other instance, other than from the perspective of the unrepentant oppressor, would anyone deem it fair or just that the abuser dictate the timeline of full liberation of the one(s) they abuse.

Anti-Racism 4REALS recognizes that racism must be interrupted in the moment, that the momentum and compounding consequences of the expressions of racism have power beyond any single infraction. Just as an object in motion stays in motion without interference, so also does any oppression intertwined with the status quo and historic preservation. This also means that those of us who are white will use anything at our disposal as weapons with which to stave off both the need for us to change and the accountability necessary for us to do so. We are the momentum that sustains and protects racism every single time and in every single way that we obstruct the work of anti-racism—including but not limited to defiling the definition of respect or mutilating what it means to meet each other where we are. In order for white people to do the work of anti-racism, we must override our instinctual and well-honed desires to dictate the timeline by which racism will be interrupted and instead interrupt racism in the moment—every time that it occurs. As with the mocha-chip ice cream scenario, if your foot has been trampled on, then regardless of the intention or even the comfort of the abuser, your foot still needs attention. You need to get to the emergency room—and doing so shouldn't be based on the timeline of the abuser's need to finish his ice cream.

With that said, here are some scenarios in which racism occurs in everyday settings. After each scenario, I'll list some options for white people to interrupt and dismantle racism in REAL TIME. In the ACTION-NOW Learning Engagement for this chapter, you'll find some common expressions of racism with space for you to script your own REAL TIME scripts and responses.

Scenario 1: *During a meeting, a Black woman speaks up about the lack of diversity within the organization. After the meeting, she and many others within the same organization received an email from a white participant stating the Black woman was* "volatile, hostile, and racist" *for constantly speaking about the need for more diverse representation within the organization.*

- If any of this language, "volatile, hostile, racist," comes up during the meeting, the interruption must happen during the meeting. If it occurs only in the email, respond to the email.

- "Reply all" with your anti-racism interruption. The racism happened in public (not privately between the speaker in the meeting and the sender of the email), so the anti-racism response should be public as well. (Refer back to pages 7-9 for an anti-racist interpretation of the "address the wrong-doer in private" story.)

- The following is a possible script for your email:

To [NAME],

I was in the aforementioned meeting and witnessed none of the behavior descriptions you mention. Rather, Ms./Mr./Title [LAST NAME] did the organization a great service by highlighting our lack of diversity and our need for change. Furthermore, naming racism as a BIPAL person is extra work they shouldn't have to do because of the way that racism targets them. Naming the problem of racism is not racist. Your email perpetrates racism by disparaging a BIPAL person with racialized stereotypes and the charge of racism. This should be rescinded with a "reply all" apology to Ms./Mr./Title [LAST NAME] forthwith.

Scenario 2: *A Research I university created a faculty search committee comprising a Black woman professor, a white woman professor, a white male professor early in his career, and two students—a Black male student from the seminary for which the faculty search was being conducted, and a white woman Ph.D. student from the religion department. Candidates were interviewed for the first round using Zoom. During one of the "see where we are" brainstorming sessions among the search committee, each committee member was identifying candidates to advance to the second round. The white male professor had no problem identifying each white candidate's credentials. When it came to assessing a Black Caribbean male candidate who had the same qualifications as one of the white male candidates, he said that he didn't think the candidate would be a good fit.*

- Name what you see: "I noticed you have a much easier time naming the credentials of each of the white candidates than those of BIPAL candidates."

- Ask specifically what he means by "don't think he would be a good fit." Oftentimes, language like this euphemizes racist statements. Asking for specific examples of why this BIPAL candidate wouldn't be a good fit requires the white male professor to (try to) name what this euphemism is covering.

- Name the specific qualifications that the Black Caribbean candidate has in common with one of the white male candidates and ask specifically what has created the difference between the two candidates for him regarding fit.

- The more specifically you ask, the closer you will get to the racism behind the euphemism.

- In addition, point out that "not a good fit" is often used in white-dominant environments to exclude BIPAL people, BIPAL candidates for hire, or BIPAL candidates for promotion. This is a specific racist statement that should be interrupted in addition to anything else that comes from having to address the euphemism.

Scenario 3: *A group of Black people bring a grievance to the CEO of the company that spells out the inequity in distribution of funding and salaries to areas that have predominantly BIPAL people. The CEO meets with the group to listen to their ideas and calls their ideas "problematic." The CEO then rolls out the newly named "CEO Initiative" which outlines all the "problematic" ideas—now described as anti-racist—as his own, without giving the group of Black people credit.*

- Respond to the rollout in the same format in which it comes. If it is sent in an email, respond in an email. If it is introduced at a press conference, respond at the press conference. If it is presented in a Zoom meeting, then respond during the presentation.

- As soon as the plagiarism occurs, interrupt it and name it for what it is. Name the specific items of the "CEO-named initiative" that have copied strategies and content from the document created by the group of Black people: "Excuse me, that exact strategy/wording comes directly from the [NAME] initiative brought to you by the [NAME] group just last week. You're stealing their work and calling it anti-racism."

- Point out that the CEO identified these strategies as problematic when they came to him from Black people, but now he's using them as if they are his strategies without citing them. This is a function of white supremacy, appropriation, and entitlement. Ask in what way he will compensate the group for their ideas and strategies.

- Require an apology, the proper citing, and that compensation be made to the group, and hold the CEO accountable for doing these things. Involve HR, social media, or other publicity forums if necessary.

BECKFORD'S RESPONSE: In this season of calling out, calling in, and cancel culture, REAL TIME is about calling a person in—but not how you may think.

- **CALLING OUT:** The term calling out is an action step used literally to call out oppressive and appalling actions and behaviors. It has become more and more prevalent as oppressive behaviors have become increasingly publicized. Social media has made it easier to call people out—and thus call for justice. Some callouts lead to individual and institutional change—some lead to people being "canceled."

- **CANCEL CULTURE:** Calling for boycotting businesses or some action such as resignations, firing from positions, and so on.

Cancel culture, historically in the hands of powerful men, has been used as a tool of revenge mostly against women who have defied or denied their advances. As a deputy of anti-Blackness racism, it is also known as blackballing or blacklisting. This culture of canceling is not new. Ancient and recent history shows us we are quick to persecute those perceived to be different, strange, or threats to power. If we are honest, it was cancel culture that executed many BIPAL leaders, and suspends or fires many in the corporate sector for requiring or pursuing cultural change. However, this tactic wielded by BIPAL people or our "allies" produces a different outcome. Rather than for revenge, cancel culture is used as a tool for accountability for racist and oppressive behavior.

REAL TIME ANTI-RACISM IN THE MEETING

During a meeting at a large conference where a group of mostly white moderates were in attendance, a prominent white author stood before the crowded room. While speaking about a group of African delegates, he said, "We invited them here to discuss the issue. We bought them pizza. The whole time we were talking to them, all they did was shake their heads. I do not know if they even understood what I was saying. I think they were just here for the pizza."

A Black woman stood up to speak about the harm that those words carried. At that point, another white facilitator stood up and asked that the conversation continue in private. The Black woman responded, "No! You said this in public; we will deal with this in public." She went on to identify the harmful words and educate those in attendance as to why the words were harmful. After she was heard, there were a number of white people who approached her and thanked her. They expressed that they knew the words were wrong, but did not know what to say to confront the racism.

For many in the field of anti-racism, *calling in* means pulling people to the side when a racial offense has happened in public. Do not "embarrass" or "challenge" the person in public, people say. Approach the offender with professionalism and respect, they say. Yet, these strategies often protect the racism that anti-racism claims to dismantle. When 4REALS uses the term *calling in*, however, we mean that racism committed in public must be addressed in public. REAL TIME calls for the interruption of racism in the moment.

REAL TIME requires accountability and education.

(REAL TALK: Please understand that it is not the obligation of BIPAL people to educate white people on racism, however, we can very well call it out.)

Although many approve of the method but lack the skills to interrupt racism in REAL TIME, there are some who disapprove. This is nothing new to me or to 4REALS. While leading workshops, we encounter vehement opposition to this REAL often. One white woman responded, "You expect me to interrupt someone while they are talking in front of everyone to let them know they said something racist. Sorry, I will not be doing that! I will not embarrass anyone." Our response was to ask her which is worse: to be a BIPAL person who is devalued, dismissed, embarrassed, and denigrated while others' silence indicates acceptance of this behavior, or to stop the harm in its tracks so everyone will know it is unacceptable.

This disapproval can be found in BIPAL communities as well. I have been challenged by a Black man who shared the following: "I would have pulled him to the side instead of embarrassing him in front of others." The person that I challenged was a white executive manager, so I am not sure whether the statement was made in respect to his title or for the purpose of coddling white manipulation (fragility). Either way, it was protecting the offender.

For many of us who operate out of good conscience and a humane ethic, the disapproval of REAL TIME interruption stems from a misinterpretation of the "address the wrongdoer in private" story, introduced on pages 7-9. We search for examples of character and leadership in those who have great power but choose not to wield it to gain leverage, advantage, or revenge. We revel in stories where those in power choose to use it for the sake of the vulnerable or to confront those who abuse their power for their own gain. But often, we are found wanting—having no recourse or skill set to enact them.

The following represent some everyday scenarios of racism. After each scenario, I've highlighted aspects of the racism perpetrated and interruptions to dismantle them.

Scenario 1: *During a meeting, a Black woman speaks up about the lack of diversity within the organization. After the meeting, she and many others within the same organization received an email from a white participant stating the Black woman was "volatile, hostile, and racist" for constantly speaking about the need for more diverse representation within the organization.*

To start off, the root of the problem is the lack of BIPAL representation in the ideas, culture, and daily operations of the company. The lack of diversity gives way to repressive silence. The ethos of the company is based in whiteness.

The use of a group email leverages shame to garner support for the author's position. Calling the Black woman "volatile, hostile, and racist" is dog-whistling code for "angry Black woman," which capitalizes on a racial stereotype. Attempting to make white people the victim in this scenario is gaslighting.

Interrupting the Racism: "Reply all" to the email and identify the racism in the original email. Close the email by restating the issue that was raised at the meeting and the facts to support it. Do not apologize for the behavior of the sender of the email. Hold the white person accountable without making excuses or implying intent. Demand the sender of the email "reply all" with a full and unconditional apology to the Black woman.

Scenario 2: *A corporate group that includes people across lines of racial difference is taking an intercultural competency workshop. They engage in the following exercise: Each participant is asked to name their favorite food their family makes at holidays or special celebrations. Then they are asked to share with the group who in their family is known for making it, how it came to be a part of their family's traditions, and how it represents their culture. After everyone shares, the facilitator says, "Each one of us has different traditions that are important to us based in our culture, but all of us share the experience of how food brings us all together. By focusing not on what makes us different but what makes us alike, we can build the bridges necessary to heal the deepest divisions among us."*

In 2017 Pepsi aired a commercial featuring Kendall Jenner. The commercial's backdrop was a group protesting injustice. Kendall's character leaves her modeling photo shoot to join the protest. While walking alongside other protesters, she fist-bumps a participant, then walks out of the crowd to a line of police officers, opens a can of Pepsi, and offers it to one of the officers. After drinking from the open can, the police officer then turns to his colleague and smiles. Kendall returns to the protestors, and everyone cheers as if this can of Pepsi fixes the racialized terror that made the protest necessary. Pepsi mistakenly centers itself as the "shared experience that brings us all together," just like the food in the intercultural competency workshop. Neither Pepsi nor the food erases the history and harm of racism. Workshops, even those that are deemed interculturally competent and that claim this is true, perpetuate racism instead.

Interrupting the Racism: This training is palatable and digestible to those who wish to deny that racism is a dividing factor. What this scenario suggests is that if we do not focus on racism, it will miraculously go away. It does not get to the root of the issue, it erases the differences of each participant, and it relegates the brilliance of human difference to happenstance. Refuse, at all costs, the temptation to take comfort only in our similarities. Rather, name the specifics of difference as assets and the ways they are used as a tool of racism to harm.

Scenario 3: *A Latina/x woman is hired as a 10th-grade teacher in a predominantly white school, located in a predominantly white school district. During a PTA meeting, she speaks out about the racism she has experienced from her fellow teachers and her students' parents. The principal of the school, a BIPAL person, diminishes her testimonial of harm by stating, "These are her experiences. This is what she thinks, but this is not an indictment against you as a school. Do you understand what I am saying?"*

What we see here is what is rarely discussed in anti-racism trainings: internalized racism. Usually, in anti-racism trainings this is not discussed because the racial identities of the participants vary. However, it exists! As BIPAL people, we are conditioned. However, as there are with most things, there are nuances to this. The above scenario displays internalized racism—a consequence of racism.

The BIPAL principal goes on to coddle the white attendees by dismissing the experiences of the Latina/x woman. His statement casts doubt on her experience in an effort to make the white attendees comfortable. His concern focuses on the false unity of the school and relieving the white people's white manipulation (fragility) at the expense of the Latina/x teacher's well-being. His comments protected the white teachers and white parents, leaving the Latina/x teacher open to more attacks because they knew at that point that she was not protected.

<u>Interrupting the Racism</u>: Teachers or parents who are aware of the racialized terror experienced by the Latina/x teacher should speak out in her defense: "I know this happened because I witnessed it." "I believe her." White-dominant schools and districts should take measures to ensure that they publicly denounce oppressive behaviors and create action steps to be taken if such occurrences of racism happen to anyone within their community.

For the teacher who was harmed, the following script could be used to address the principal, and even the superintendent of schools for that district:

> By my own testimonial—verbal and in writing in multiple settings now—I have provided ample evidence of individual, interpersonal, and institutional racism that has occurred since my start date here. (Name specific instances here.) Your insistence that the specific harm done to me is limited to "my experiences" and "not an indictment" of the school, district, or its people highlighted for me your priority to protect the false unity of the school and district over and against your duties to ensure your teachers can engage in their work without racial harassment, discrimination, or terror. I am looking for specific, concrete support from you to address the racism of the school, parents, and teachers and the harm done to me.

ACTION-NOW Learning Engagement
REAL TIME: Brainstorming Scenarios and Scripts

Below, a number of expressions of racism are named. After each example, use the lines below to [1] name the racism perpetrated and [2] write out a script you could use to interrupt that form of racism the next time you encounter it. As you write your own scripts, keep these things in mind:

- **Racism must be interrupted in the moment.** Note when in the scenario you would speak or act, how late is too late, when an interruption takes the form of silence, and how your racial identity dictates what your interruption is in each scenario. What, if any, personal hesitations that currently hold you back from interrupting racism in REAL TIME must be overcome—and how will you overcome them?

- **Anti-racism must be enacted immediately after learning what to do/not to do.** What learning or experiences of anti-racism inform the content as well as the method you use to interrupt racism? If you do not interrupt racism in the moment, make sure to prepare for the next time by researching, planning, and role-playing your anti-racism response.

- **Anti-racists must see preparation and practice as necessary to get ready, be ready, and stay ready.** We *do not* re-enact racism, especially in groups across racial difference. Role-playing the racism creates the harm of racism. For people who are unfamiliar with a particular form of racism or who have trouble recognizing it in the moment, Google it. Unfortunately, plenty of examples can be found with a simple search.

- **For those of us who are white:** We must always consider it our responsibility to interrupt racism in REAL TIME unless directed not to do so by a BIPAL person or strategy.

- **For BIPAL people:** Our responsibility is not to shield, protect, or try to explain away the racism or harm in each scenario.

WRITE YOUR RESPONSE: *What are two ways you will overcome a personal hesitation to interrupting racism in real time in the coming week?*

Scenario 1: *An Asian woman attends a town hall meeting that was called to discuss ways to "create organizational unity." The discussion moves to COVID precautions and the ways that racism has created different health, economic, and social consequences of COVID based in racial identity. Hearing this, she specifically highlights the term "Chinese virus" as harmful and racist. She shares experiences of her own and those of her children and how isolated they feel from their community that once embraced them. She also mentions how she doesn't always know how she "fits" within conversations about racism that only talk about "Black and white."*

Scenario 2: *At an anti-racism rally, a number of leaders of social justice and other nonprofit organizations were invited to speak. A white male president of a national social justice organization was one of the speakers. He had a wide range of accomplishments on his resume and in his work as president leading a coalition made up of diverse ideologies to work together. However, he had no proven or documented evidence of anti-racism work to his credit—either vocational or personal. His speech invited all gathered to rely on love to unify us, cautioned against focusing on our differences, and highlighted exemplary people of color who have done the work of bringing people together in the face of hatred, including the Rev. Dr. Martin Luther King Jr.*

Scenario 3: *A well-known organization tapped four of their employees to represent their company at an annual meeting. A flier was distributed over social media and other venues. The description next to each employee's name and picture, except for the Pacific Islander woman, included their official title and function within the company (for example, Director of Personnel FIRST NAME LAST NAME). The Pacific Islander woman's information listed her name and marital status as if it were her title (Mrs. FIRST NAME LAST NAME), even though she was selected specifically for her skill set based on her role in the company.*

Scenario 4: *A keynote speaker (or high-level executive) says something racist during their presentation (or report/meeting) or someone tells a racist joke.*

** 4REALS-written scripts and responses to the aforementioned scenarios can be found in Appendix A on pages 117-120.

Chapter 5:

REAL CHANGE: B.E. Change

> REAL CHANGE crafts accountability templates and measures to ensure that tangible, meaningful, and powerful change for racial justice replaces good intentions and workshops. REAL CHANGE requires that we focus on outcome, not on intent. REAL CHANGE provides ways to track, assess, and analyze successes and failures (yes, failures), and make on-the-go shifts that avoid the most common roadblocks and obstacles to anti-racism work. REAL CHANGE creates methods of accountability and transparency that build not only timelines and momentum but also trust. REAL CHANGE provides the external measurements and an accountability paradigm that brings all people the opportunity to participate in anti-racism work that actually does the work of anti-racism.

Because REAL CHANGE requires action, this chapter is set up a little bit differently. Our racially positioned responses are shorter so that we can offer more space for templates of accountability, assessment, and action. We've had REAL TALK and offered REAL STRATEGIES for anti-racism work in REAL TIME. Now is the time to assess what has been done and stand accountable for what has not. Now is the time to put the words, intentions, and practice into measurable steps. Now is the time to assess whether our talk has become our walk. REAL CHANGE is where anti-racism becomes anti-racist. This chapter is set up to provide multiple ways for that to occur.

BECKFORD'S RESPONSE: The movie *One Night in Miami* inspired the subtitle for this chapter: B.E. Change. As the film title suggests, the movie takes place on one night in Miami, where four famous Black men meet in a hotel room to enjoy a historic victory. Sam Cooke (a musician), Muhammad Ali (a boxer originally named, Cassius Clay), Jim Brown (an NFL star turned actor), and the Honorable Malcolm X (a Nation of Islam civil rights activist) gather to celebrate Clay's boxing win, but that's not all. The festive evening begins with change. The hotel room where they stay is not filled with people, alcohol, loud music, or dancing, as we would expect at a celebration of an event of this magnitude. Instead, the four men share their desires, hopes, fears, and beliefs. The Honorable Malcolm X uses this entry point to speak with his friends about using the power their platforms afford them. By the final scene of the movie, each person has done just that.

The subtitle of this chapter is B.E. Change. Here, the "B.E." stands for "Beyond Excuses." In anti-racism work, every single one of us must push beyond excuses. BIPAL people are always accused of making excuses for not pulling ourselves up by our bootstraps. We are often told that we use excuses such as "we're paid less" or "the hiring practices are discriminatory" to defend why we don't advance in the workplace or in life. But 4REALS is talking about something different here. Excuses are reasons for avoiding responsibility without factual foundation. These are not excuses—these are facts based in racist policies, procedures, and practices. Structural oppression plays a major role in how our communities bang against glass ceilings. What are often categorized as excuses that BIPAL people use to avoid succeeding or thriving are actually the realities of institutional and systemic racism that we must push against in order to dislodge, disrupt, and dismantle it.

For BIPAL people, the excuses that prevent REAL CHANGE include the following:

- No one will listen to me, so there's no use in trying.

- I am a BIPAL person, so I don't need anti-racism work; by nature, I am anti-racist.

- We don't have the resources to combat whiteness.

The fact remains: If or when we do the bidding of whiteness so it can prevail, we are not anti-racist. At the same time, we are not racist because we do not have the power to uphold or change policies. However—and this is often overlooked—we can participate in racist behaviors that advance the agendas and systems that perpetrate racialized terror.

To do the kind of REAL CHANGE that goes beyond excuses, it is important that we admit to ourselves our participation in excuse-making.

BIPAL PEOPLE ONLY: Note any excuses you have used in the past that have prevented you from using your opportunities or platforms to make a difference.

White people also make excuses for why they are not engaged in anti-racism work. The reasons they often give are not grounded in systemic racism functioning to oppress white people. Thus, these are just excuses, and white people use them to excuse themselves from doing what is necessary because of discomfort, risk, manipulation, or fear. Some examples follow:

- We are not wanted in anti-racism work; we get rejected by BIPAL people when we try.

- That is not our work to do.

- We need more information/education.

- I do not know what to say or do; I say nothing to be on the safe side.

- This is how I was raised.

WHITE PEOPLE ONLY: Note all reasons you have used to excuse yourself from engaging in anti-racism work.

When we are honest with ourselves, we find that most of the things holding us back from REAL CHANGE are excuses. For BIPAL people, some of them are instead realities, based in structural racism meant to oppress us, that are misnamed as excuses, while others are actual excuses. For white people, excuses serve as defense mechanisms—to distance them from their responsibility and to protect the benefits they reap. For each of us, REAL CHANGE requires admitting our excuses as a first step. For all of us, REAL CHANGE requires us to push BEYOND EXCUSES.

LEDDER'S RESPONSE: It's one thing to talk about wanting change; it's another to do what is necessary to enact it. REAL CHANGE requires more than intent, more than slogans, more than the latest lingo, more than research, more than workshops, and more than another book study. REAL CHANGE requires a transformation, so that what has been before no longer remains.

In terms of anti-racism, REAL CHANGE is the consequence of actually interrupting and dismantling racism. REAL CHANGE can recognize, name, locate, describe, and explain with proven evidence that racism has been interrupted and/or dismantled. For this, measures of accountability, assessment, and action are necessary. For those of us who are white, this is where the proverbial rubber hits the road. If change does not occur in tangible, meaningful, and powerful ways according to BIPAL people, we are not doing anti-racism work. Thus, our claims to believe in anti-racism, to desire racism's demise, and to risk whatever it takes to stand for what is just, stand or fall based on whether REAL CHANGE has occurred.

REAL CHANGE demands proof of intentions, proof of actions, and proof of anti-racism. REAL CHANGE takes many forms, but it is extinct without evidence. White people must be capable of doing whatever needs to be done to interrupt and dismantle racism by any means necessary. We will do so by obeying the REAL STRATEGIES created or cosigned by BIPAL people, and we will implement them in REAL TIME. REAL CHANGE places all of our promises to want to do good, to do good, and to be about the good in full view and asks, "But did we do it?" REAL CHANGE refuses to allow those of us who are white to rest in any form of pretense that does not actuate anti-racism. REAL CHANGE is an accounting of our actions or inactions and will not accept plans, goals, or action steps as bond. REAL CHANGE reminds white people that we do not have the luxury of being white and not engaging in anti-racism work on a deliberate, deliverable level. REAL CHANGE exposes all of our excuses and claims that we "meant to" and calls us into accountability, responsibility, and consequence. REAL CHANGE asks us what we've been doing with all of our information gathering and listening, what risks and responsibilities we've taken, and how we've obeyed the strategies of BIPAL people. REAL TALK is just more talk without REAL CHANGE. REAL STRATEGIES are just to-do lists without REAL CHANGE. REAL TIME is just another distraction without REAL CHANGE. Anti-racism is racism in a pretty mask without REAL CHANGE.

On a scale from 1 to 10, with 1 being the least amount of work and 10 being the greatest, how much anti-racism REAL CHANGE do you believe you have enacted since you began reading this book?

1   2   3   4   5   6   7   8   9   10

Explain to someone who hasn't read the book why you answered the way you did on the previous question.

_____

_____

_____

_____

_____

Out of all the anti-racism options and strategies this book has listed thus far, what percentage do you think you've enacted since you started reading this book?

_____

_____

_____

_____

_____

How, if at all, does this align with your first answer (1–10) above?

_____

_____

_____

_____

_____

ACTION-NOW Learning Engagement:
REAL TEMPLATES FOR CHANGE

REAL CHANGE requires a sustainable revolution in policies, procedures, power, and practice, because making policy changes without enforcing them keeps the practices of oppression intact. This level of sustainability requires transparent accountability and undisputable commitment. For accountability, assessment, and action to occur, there must be a method for measurement. Anti-Racism 4REALS believes in templates that not only determine whether racism has been interrupted or dismantled but also serve as a road map for enacting the necessary work. The following set of REAL CHANGE templates creates a number of entry points for interrupting and dismantling racism and for creating accountability, transparency, and trust. The templates follow the same principles as the other ACTION-NOW Learning Engagements: You can start to use them as soon as you finish the chapter, leave the workshop, or click "leave meeting." They can be adapted for nonprofits, business corporations, schools, government agencies, start-ups, neighborhoods, and more. For more customized work, Anti-Racism 4REALS offers workshops and consulting packages to help any group use these and other custom-built templates to actualize anti-racism work.

While this is not an exhaustive list, the pages that follow provide a diverse range of opportunities to engage in anti-racism with REAL TALK and REAL STRATEGIES in REAL TIME. Each REAL CHANGE template includes instructions, nuances for contextualization, and a worksheet model for notes, plans, and accountability. Let's get started!

REAL LIST 4 REAL CHANGE

INSTRUCTIONS: In Appendix B you will find a list of anti-racism strategies, ideas, and ACTION-NOW Learning Engagements listed in *Doing Anti-Racist Business: Dislodging and Dismantling Racism with the 4REALS*. For a refresher, go to the page number(s) listed before beginning the strategy. Worksheets for notes follow serving as a template you can use to list: [1] how you have enacted this strategy thus far; [2] what internal or external resistance you have experienced regarding this strategy; [3] what your plan is to enact this strategy; [4] to whom you will be accountable for enacting this strategy; or [5] what this strategy's contextualized interruption and dismantling of racism in your organization, community, school, business, or otherwise will be. Utilize this ACTION-NOW Learning Engagement to track your anti-racism work and to create a longer-term anti-racist anti-racism strategy.

Name of Strategy:

Pages:

How have you used this strategy thus far?

What internal or external resistance have you experienced regarding this strategy?

What is your plan for enacting this strategy?

Who will be accountable to whom for enacting this strategy? How does this follow the overall template for doing anti-racism work (BIPAL people create or cosign strategy, white people enact all of it except specific actions designated for only BIPAL people, and white people are accountable to BIPAL people to determine obedience to strategy and effectiveness of work)?

Name of Strategy:

Pages:

How have you used this strategy thus far?

What internal or external resistance have you experienced re-garding this strategy?

What is your plan for enacting this strategy?

Who will be accountable to whom for enacting this strategy? How does this follow the overall template for doing anti-racism work (BIPAL people create or cosign strategy, white people enact all of it except specific actions designated for only BIPAL people, and white people are accountable to BIPAL people to determine obedience to strategy and effectiveness of work)?

Name of Strategy: _____

Pages: _____

How have you used this strategy thus far?

What internal or external resistance have you experienced regarding this strategy?

What is your plan for enacting this strategy?

Who will be accountable to whom for enacting this strategy? How does this follow the overall template for doing anti-racism work (BIPAL people create or cosign strategy, white people enact all of it except specific actions designated for only BIPAL people, and white people are accountable to BIPAL people to determine obedience to strategy and effectiveness of work)?

Name of Strategy:

Pages:

How have you used this strategy thus far?

What internal or external resistance have you experienced regarding this strategy?

What is your plan for enacting this strategy?

Who will be accountable to whom for enacting this strategy? How does this follow the overall template for doing anti-racism work (BIPAL people create or cosign strategy, white people enact all of it except specific actions designated for only BIPAL people, and white people are accountable to BIPAL people to determine obedience to strategy and effectiveness of work)?

30 THINGS ANTI-RACISTS SHOULD STOP DOING RIGHT NOW

1. Stop asking one BIPAL person to explain how all people within their racial identity think about, value, believe, or do something.

2. Stop holding all people within a BIPAL racial identity accountable for the actions of one person with the same racial identity.

3. Stop trying to achieve equality when the anti-racist goal is equity.

4. Stop all forms of racialized salary discrimination practices.

5. Stop equating the term "professional" with standards of whiteness.

6. Stop using racial quotas to cover up inequitable hiring practices.

7. Stop using the word "diversity" to minimize racialized inequity.

8. Stop stealing ideas, strategies, and work from BIPAL people and attributing them to white people.

9. Stop equating people who call out racism with people who are "too sensitive" or "troublemakers."

10. For white people: Stop using the term "allowing" when in discussions or meetings with BIPAL people. For example, "I'll allow you to speak now."

11. Stop saying, "It's not that big of a deal" when someone names racism or microaggressions that have occurred.

12. Stop saying, "Was it *really* racism?" when someone calls out racism or microaggressions that have occurred.

13. Stop hiring people who cannot provide external evidence of their anti-racism work.

14. Stop creating anti-racism policies that are not enforced with accountability and consequences.

15. Stop equating intercultural competency (or diversity or inclusion) with anti-racism.

16. Stop forcing BIPAL people to serve on anti-racism committees without reasonable compensation (for example, adjusting current portfolio or adding salary).

17. Stop creating anti-racist policies (or a task force) without the input of BIPAL people.

18. For white people: Stop waiting until after the meeting to tell BIPAL people how offended you were at the racism that occurred during the meeting.

19. Stop pitting BIPAL people against each other.

20. Stop pretending as if all examples of racism within your organization are the anomaly and not part of a larger system.

21. Stop including language in your training materials that urges employees to ignore racialized differences (for example, "we're all the same here" or "we see everyone as...").

22. Stop creating different prerequisites for hire, promotion, and salary increases based in racial identity of a candidate/ employee.

23. Stop equating representation with racial equity.

24. Stop allowing internal departments to conduct racial equity audits for your organization.

25. Stop equating tokenism with racialized diversity.

26. Stop using the term "diversity hire" and learn why it's important to do so.

27. Stop using phrases such as "effective leadership," "culture fit," and "safe space" to cover up racist policies, practices, and procedures.

28. Stop allowing employees to use racial stereotypes and microaggressions without accountability and consequences.

29. Stop allowing executive leadership to remain in place without external evidence of anti-racism work.

30. Stop equating anti-racism workshops with an anti-racist organizational culture.

Here's a list of five things you can replace RIGHT NOW to interrupt and dismantle racism by using the logic system of anti-racism.

QUICK REPLACEMENT LIST:

Replace This	With This	Anti-Racist Logic
The term "minority"	The term "minoritized"	BIPAL people are statistically the global majority. Racism attempts to decenter BIPAL people by creating socio-political misnomers.
The term and practices of "diversity hires"	The term and practices of "racially equitable hiring"	The term "diversity hire" limits hiring practices to representational models and protects tokenism as well as negative racialized biases regarding merit and skill.
Internal equity audits	Equity audits conducted by BIPAL-owned external firms	BIPAL people are the best equipped to recognize and name racism. External firms are best equipped to recognize what organizations take for granted, overlook, or protect.
Defining "professionalism" using standards of whiteness	Explicitly define "professionalism" by naming goals rather than prioritizing specific expressions of how those goals are enacted.	When definitions of terms are assumed and not explicitly defined, all the stereotypes, biases, and racism of the person using the terms are loaded into them. Ensure that specific goals are named and learn how different racialized expressions enact them.
"Bad Apples" excuses (as if racism is limited to one person or policy)	Addressing how experiences of racism reflect the larger organizational culture	Anti-Racist business culture requires accountability measures versus excuses for anomalies. Create and enforce policies and practices that focus on accountability and consequences for doing or not doing business aligned with anti-racism outcomes.

Job Posting Summary

About (Company Name):

(Company Name) is on a beautiful campus, including three satellite offices in the Northeast Corridor. It has a total of 3,000 employees, including a 20-person Board of Directors and a 10-person C-Suite Team. Over 30% of our employees are from underrepresented groups and minorities. We were honored in 2021 to learn we have been ranked 16th in our field for international diversity hires. We deeply respect the work-life balance of our employees and continuously work to ensure that everyone within the (Company Name) family feels like a part of the team.

Before going any further, take five to ten minutes to name aspects of the "about us" job summary description that perpetrates the logic and language of racism. (There are at least five.)

The original "about us" summary is littered with "red flags." This company attempts to hide its racism behind charismatic words. Anti-Racism 4REALS recognizes this as racism "hiding in plain sight." Even though the wording sounds inclusive and appealing, racism sits behind a façade. However, when anti-racism logic and analysis are applied to it, the charade is revealed. We have highlighted aspects of the "about us" job summary description that perpetrate the logic and language of racism. Compare your list to our findings below. How did you do?

(Company Name) is on a beautiful campus, including three satellite offices in the Northeast Corridor. It has a total of <u>3,000 employees, including a 20-person Board of Directors and a 10-person C-Suite Team.</u> Over 30% of our employees are from <u>underrepresented</u> groups and <u>minorities.</u> We were honored in 2021 to learn we have been ranked 16th in our field for <u>international diversity hires.</u> We deeply respect the work-life balance of our employees and continuously work to ensure that everyone within the (Company Name) <u>family</u> feels like <u>a part of the team.</u>

Using anti-racism language and logic, we have transformed the original posting to reflect an anti-racist assessment for the "about us" summary job description. This does not transform the company into an anti-racist company. Rather, it imagines possible realities that reflect the truth about the original posting.

(Company Name) is on a beautiful campus, including three satellite offices in the Northeast Corridor. It has a total of 3,000 employees, including a 20-person Board of Directors and a 10-person C-Suite Team. We affirm diversity and strive for inclusion. Our employee makeup: 85% white, 10% Asian, 2% Black, 0.2% Indigenous, 0.8% Latino/x, 4% identify as Other. Our Board of Directors is 90% white, 2% Asian, 2% Black, 1% Latino/x. We were honored in 2021 to learn we have been ranked 16th in our field for international diversity hires, with 75% Korean people, 20% European women, 1% African people, 3.6% Chinese people, and 0.4% Brazilian people. We promote work-life balance in the workplace by honoring a diverse array of religious holidays and promoting a two-day-per-week work-from-home option.

ANTI-RACISM INTERVIEW QUESTIONS

To do anti-racist business, interviewers must eradicate racism from the hiring process (interrogate all implicit and explicit biases for anti-racist outcomes) and construct anti-racist hiring practices. Each requires a different skill set (removing/transforming and adding/building). For this ACTION-NOW Learning Engagement, Anti-Racism 4REALS offers ten questions to ask in interviews that act as catalysts to discern the anti-racism prowess of your candidates. Organizations capable of doing anti-racist business must have employees capable of doing anti-racist business. By ensuring that you hire candidates with sharply honed anti-racist skills, value sets, and agility, your company is primed to create, grow, and sustain an anti-racist organizational culture.

A couple of notes about compliance:

- These questions, and others you might use, must not serve to force candidates to offer your organization free anti-racism labor. In other words, any questions asked or scenarios posed must not be used to create anti-racism policies, procedures, practices or structures. Rather, the purpose of the questions is to ascertain the depth and breadth of the candidate's anti-racism skills, value-base, and agility and how these connect with the open job position.[21]

- Help your HR department understand how these questions are not biased, even though they ask candidates to talk specifically about race, racism, and anti-racism.[22]

  — Each question you ask in interviews must be asked of all candidates.

---

[21]See also, "The Working Job Interviews that Go Too Far." Accessed August 31, 2021.

[22]Anti-Racism 4REALS is not a legal consultant nor HR firm. Our focus centers on how to create anti-racist organizational culture and how to do the work of anti-racism. Many HR groups and consultants suggest avoiding all questions about race and "color" to avoid enacting discriminatory interview and hiring practices. The one caveat includes "bona-fide occupational qualifications." In this case, we are arguing that to build an anti-racist organizational culture your employees, at all levels, must possess anti-racism skills, value-sets, and agility. In this way we argue that employees must have opportunities to provide evidence of that – in this case, with some of the interview questions. We have offered additional notation on information you can bring to your HR or legal department but do not infer, at any level, legal counsel. In addition to bringing these matters to your HR or legal team, Anti-Racism 4REALS suggests you determine a method to discern whether they are relying on older models which categorically dismiss questions of race, racism, or anti-racism, or whether they, themselves, are skilled in anti-racism and can discern which anti-racism questions are legal and non-discriminatory.

- Each question (listed here) avoids relying on or asking about stereotypes of any kind, specifically race.

- Each question (listed here) does not replicate any form of racism. Rather, questions are meant to elicit responses of anti-racism. (Similar to REAL TIME imperatives to avoid role-playing racism scenarios, pages 65-66)

Write here your initial concerns about asking interview questions that serve to create, grow, and sustain an anti-racist organizational culture:

ANTI-RACISM INTERVIEW QUESTIONS

1. How do you define anti-racism?

2. How does your racial identity help you navigate working in an organization committed to building and sustaining a culture of anti-racism?

3. Explain the difference between Intercultural Competency and Anti-Racism.

4. What connections do you see between anti-racism and this job/field/discipline?

5. Recall a time when you confronted or challenged racism in your workplace. What did you do to interrupt and dismantle racism? How do you know what you did was anti-racist?

6. How has your prior anti-racism work prepared you specifically for this job?

7. How has your prior anti-racism work prepared you specifically to help build an anti-racist organizational culture here?

8. What challenges are you currently addressing to help strengthen your anti-racism work?

9. How do you discern whether the decisions you're making or the strategies you're creating are anti-racist?

10. Name one anti-racism action or strategy you have enacted in prior job positions. Please include the external evidence that shows how the action or strategy was actually anti-racist.

CREATING A MORE RACIALLY EQUITABLE BOARD OR LEADERSHIP GROUP

When white-dominant organizations recognize their need for a more racially diverse board or leadership group, models of "diversity" and "inclusion" fall short by doing harm in many ways—including perpetrating more racism. The ACTION-NOW Learning Engagement below will help you identify the current thinking strategies of your organization and provide a five-step (and a bonus for start-ups) anti-racist anti-racism template to honorably create a more racially equitable board or leadership group.

ACTION-NOW Learning Engagement:

You can do this exercise alone, with a group, or with a set of small groups.

Imagine you are creating a racially equitable twelve-member board or leadership group for your nonprofit, social justice group, organization, school, or business. Think very specifically about race, the racial identities of the members, the racial demographics of the surrounding community, the history of your group and its leadership, and the qualifications for leadership you want the members to have. Take between five and fifteen minutes to brainstorm and list the racialized makeup of the new board or leadership group. Be prepared to discuss with others how you came up with the list and how you would make the changes between the current all-white or white-dominant group and the new one. Include also, if you can, how decisions were anti-racist.

After brainstorming and creating your list, answer the following prompts.

List the racial makeup of the group.

How did you decide the new racial makeup of the group?

What about the new racial makeup makes this more equitable board/ leadership group anti-racist?

What about your process and/or the new racial makeup makes the process honorable?

CREATING A MORE RACIALLY EQUITABLE BOARD
OR LEADERSHIP GROUP: DEBRIEF

In all the times Anti-Racism 4REALS has facilitated this ACTION-NOW Learning Engagement not one time did a group create and describe a board or leadership group that was 100 percent BIPAL people. Not once. This includes groups who have a well-documented and known history of boards/leadership groups that have been 100 percent white for over 100 years. Consider again the equality model versus the equity model. Equity addresses past and current inequality but doesn't use equality models to address it. Racialized equitable boards and leadership groups will use methods that don't seem "fair" according to the equality model (in which every share/risk/opportunity is of equal measure). Rather, equity requires justice, and justice requires new percentages and strategies that cannot make up for past and current inequality, but that begin to make some recompense for discriminatory practices and harm.

Five Action Items to Honorably Create a More Racially Equitable Board or Leadership Group

1. Require all current board/leadership group members to submit their resignations and reapply for selection. Rewrite selection criteria to require proven evidence of anti-racism work. Anti-racism work will include BIPAL people's lived experiences resisting racism directed at them and their communities.

2. Determine the number of years the board/leadership group has been in existence. Determine an average number of members of each board/group. Multiply these together. Determine to the best of your ability the number of BIPAL people who have served thus far in your organization's history. Subtract the number of BIPAL people from the total to calculate how many terms white people have served. How many terms would the board have to consist of 100 percent BIPAL people before the number of white people's terms and BIPAL people's terms were equal? (See page 104 for worksheet.)

3. What excuses would you have to refute or counter if the new policy were to mandate 100 percent BIPAL people on the board/in the leadership group for the next five years?

4. Create time, agenda structure, and the priorities of the board/leadership group meetings based on guidance from BIPAL people in your organization.

5. Pay or increase salary for all BIPAL people for their board/leadership group service. Refute or counter claims that no one gets paid for their service with the following argument:

a. No one gets paid for the work of the board (whatever that is).

b. BIPAL people are being paid for additional work they do on top of what everyone is doing as their board/leadership group service. This work includes the following:

  i. racially diversifying the group (BIPAL people are required for this to occur—this is something white people cannot do on their own.)

  ii. withstanding the harm of micro- and macro-aggressions while the white members learn anti-racism

  iii. teaching the white members about anti-racism, including but not limited to the racism the white members enact (also enduring white members' white manipulation (fragility).)

  iv. creating or cosigning anti-racist anti-racism strategies for the board/leadership group to engage as practice or policy or organization

6. **BONUS FOR START-UPS:** Since your group will be selecting its first Board of Directors or leadership group, you'll be setting the anti-racist example from the start versus having to replace or edit the current board or leadership group.

a. List the first qualification for board/leadership service/membership as externally evidenced anti-racism work. This should be stated first, as its own category and before any content-related or other qualifications such as education or leadership skills.

b. For BIPAL candidates, externally evidenced anti-racism work will also include the work they do to resist racism, because they, themselves, are directly targeted by racism.

c. Determine ahead of time and explicitly what number or percentage of BIPAL people will serve on this board/group. (51 percent is BIPAL-led, 75 percent would be considered BIPAL dominant, 100 percent would move significantly toward equity and set a distinct standard of addressing historic and current precedent industry-wide. (Here, it doesn't matter what industry you are in, it will apply.)

d. Consider creating voting strategies that prioritize the votes of BIPAL board or leadership group members. For example, if the BIPAL members are unanimous in their vote, the motion/policy passes/is approved no matter the number of votes from white members.

Five Action Steps to Honorably Create a More Racially Equitable Board or Leadership Group

*this ACTION-NOW Learning Engagement assumes one-year board terms.

	Example
1. Number of years the board or leadership group has been in existence	100
2. Average number of members on the board at a time	10
3. Multiply to get the number of "spots" available until now	100 x 10 = 1,000
4. Number of BIPAL people who have served thus far in the organization's history	5
5. Subtract the number of terms BIPAL people have served	(4) 2 for 2 years (3) 3 for 1 year 7 terms

Total "spots" (1,000) minus BIPAL terms (7) = 993

Thus, 99 years of 100% BIPAL terms to "catch up."

DEVELOPING AN EQUITY MODEL

Equity works to repair the historic, ongoing, and compounding harm of racism and racialized discrimination. Equity models serve as guideposts, accountability templates, and interpretive lenses by which organizations of any sort can create racial equity in policy, procedure, practice, and power. The following ten questions can get you started. Your answers provide the entry points both for goals and for the work needed to get you there.

1. What is the difference between equality and equity?

2. How does this model decenter whiteness?

3. How does this model ensure that racially equitable policies are adhered to regardless of an individual's personal stance?

4. How does the makeup of your board represent ongoing racism or an anti-racism culture? (To begin, create a list of the names and titles of the most powerful decision-makers in your organization. Next to each name write the person's racial identity.)

5. How many policies have been written from the lens of anti-racism? How do you know?

6. How do you measure pay equity? How are issues of pay inequity remedied?

7. What is necessary to remove all implicit and explicit racialized bias from the position, promotion, and leadership requirements of your organization?

8. What process is necessary to identify and remove all racialized bias from your organizational training and onboarding?

9. What policies and accountability are in place to ensure that leaders of your organization have proven evidence of anti-racism training, skills, and outcomes?

10. What five things can you do right now to create a foundation of anti-racism culture in your organization that reflects equity?

CREATE AN ANTI-RACIST BUDGET

It has been said that if we want to know what is important to a person or organization, we should look at their budget. This is because we spend and allocate our money to that which we deem worthy. Budgets can perpetrate racism explicitly and implicitly—from money spent to fund racially unjust endeavors, to charitable donations, to vendor decisions. Use the checklist below to create a budget using anti-racist strategies with an anti-racist lens. Start with an existing budget or create one anew.

Prompt questions:

1. How does your organization vet vendors?

    • What does it mean to be an anti-racist organization?

    • How would you know whether an organization is anti-racist?

    • A company based in a racially diverse city has fifteen employees, only two of whom are BIPAL people who hold managerial positions. There are no other BIPAL employees. Does this fit an anti-racist model? No. A seven-to-one ratio isn't anti-racist.

    • A company based in a white community with two BIPAL families has fifteen employees, one of whom is a BIPAL person. Does this fit an anti-racist model? It could! Even though in this example there is only one person instead of two, based on the racial demographics of the community the representation of BIPAL people is statistically higher. Additional questions should include whether the BIPAL person is expected to conform to the standards of whiteness (for example, repressive silence).

2. Have BIPAL people contributed to the creation of your budget?

    • If not, why not? What excuses have been used to justify this?

    • Name the racial identities of the people on your budget committees.

    • How do you know the strategies and priorities of BIPAL people are honored in your budget?

3. Is there funding for anti-racism work?

    • How do you define anti-racism work? What qualifies?

    • Specifically, what percentage of your budget contributes directly to creating and protecting an anti-racism culture in your company?

- Who makes the final decisions about funding? What, if any, changes need to be made?

4. Is there racial equity in salaries?

   - Review the current salaries and disaggregate (separate by component parts) by race.

   - Determine the difference between equality and equity. Use the model that addresses past and current inequalities in salary based on race.

   - Readjust budget accordingly.

5. Transfer or switch all financial accounts to economic institutions run by and/or owned by BIPAL people.

   - Transfer your credit cards, bank accounts, mortgages, and investments.

   - White people: Avoid opening or transferring accounts to BIPAL-owned credit unions, especially Black-owned credit unions. Credit unions are owned by the account holders. Flooding the credit union with accounts owned by white people changes the ownership status.

CONCLUSION

There is no half-hearted solution that will dislodge, disrupt, and dismantle racism. Yes, 4REALS has spent the entirety of these pages introducing entry points to challenge everyone into action right now. We do this to refute the lie that some people aren't ready, or that anti-racism prerequisites must be satisfied before doing something, or that the work is so great that silence or unresponsiveness is acceptable. If anything, for us, this speaks to the reality that racism, and the work to dismantle it, is enormous, entrenched, and escalating. Racism is brutality levied against BIPAL people *so that* those of us who are white may survive, thrive, and succeed at their expense.

WRITE YOUR RESPONSE: *What was your initial response to the last sentence? Especially consider your logical, emotional, and physical reaction to the words "so that."*

WHITE PEOPLE, WRITE YOUR RESPONSE: *Record internal or explicit counterarguments that come up for you here. After doing so, write down which aspect of racism is connected to each counterargument. What do you need to do to interrupt and dismantle your attachment to this aspect of racism?*

Counterargument	Aspect of Racism	Dismantle Attachment

Although entry points and REAL STRATEGIES provide multiple opportunities for anyone to do the work of anti-racism right now, it's equally important to stay focused on the system of racism and how it functions. To do so, we must hold two major categories in tandem. Racism has many expressions, and examples can be discussed using two overarching categories. **Individual or interpersonal racism** focuses on beliefs, values, and actions held within a person or expressed within a relationship (either professional or personal). **Institutional or systemic racism** focuses on policies, practices, and procedures that perpetrate racism within an institution (such as religious institutions, the American banking system, or higher education) or across institutions (for example, racialized discrimination in banking affects who receives mortgages, which affects who builds home equity, which affects local school funding and higher education choices).

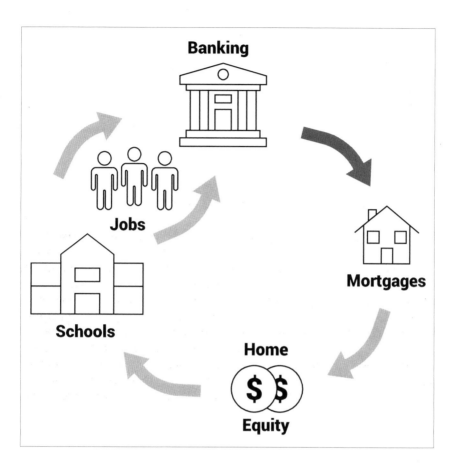

Both categories must be addressed. The constant call for society to shift before business policies can change *sounds* good. However, addressing institutional/systemic racism without addressing individual/ interpersonal racism can lead to hypocrisy—policies on paper that don't interrupt racist decisions, or promotions based in the racialized discrimination coded in language like "managerial discretion" or "culture fit." Changing policies without changing those in power only drives people to find creative ways to circumvent the new policies. The logic of racism surmises that we must focus on individual and interpersonal racism for institutional/systemic anti-racism to stick. Furthermore, especially in white-dominant groups, the focus shifts solely to the individual/interpersonal work *until* people have been prepared to create and protect the changes necessary for institutional/systemic equity and justice. But here's the thing:

> **_There is no automatic pathway between individual/interpersonal anti-racism and institutional/systemic anti-racism._**

Any business committed to doing anti-racism work must start with the institutional/systemic without neglecting the individual/interpersonal.

REAL TALK: Did you think that this was going to be just another book study? You have read through each chapter of *Doing Anti-Racist Business: Dislodging and Dismantling Racism with the 4REALS: REAL TALK with REAL STRATEGIES in REAL TIME for REAL CHANGE*. However, anti-racist anti-racism work requires that each of us applies the ACTION-NOW Learning Engagements and other strategies found within these pages to our REAL lives.

WRITE YOUR RESPONSE: *Have you ever been told to write the significant facts or points of a book in the margins so you can go back to them? We ask that you go back to those initial feelings, beliefs, and questions you had as you read through this book. Next, identify the areas or times in your life where you participated in racial discrimination or perpetrated racism.*

Absorbing information *about* anti-racism without *application of* anti-racism is useless. To engage with this book as just another book study without applying the information learned is a waste of time and wisdom. Take a moment to use the strategy of practice to commit to making anti-racism and using the 4REALS a daily practice and lifelong work. Two options to begin follow.

The first is a commitment letter written by you to yourself. Add specifics based on your racial positionality and how it influences how you will honorably do the work of anti-racism.

Dear _____ ,

I have read the book *Doing Anti-Racist Business: Disrupting and Dismantling Racism with the 4REALS* and committed to practice the strategies I've learned while engaging in anti-racism work. I recognize that I have practiced, perpetrated, or participated in actions or inactions rooted in white supremacy. These actions furthered the harm caused to BIPAL people (or to my community, for BIPAL people). I will continue to use these anti-racism strategies generally:

1. _____ ,

2. _____ ,

3. _____ .

In order to specifically dislodge, disrupt, and dismantle racism *in my personal life*, I commit to the following anti-racist strategies:

1. _____ ,

2. _____ ,

3. _____ .

I also commit to these strategies specifically to dislodge, disrupt, and dismantle racism *within systems*:

1. _____ ,

2. _____ ,

3. _____ ,

or _____ .

When I falter, because I will, I will hold myself accountable by moving beyond excuses to correct my actions and apologize to those I have harmed. I understand that these next steps will require resistance, resiliency, courage, and—in some cases—consequences, yet I commit myself to doing this critical and necessary work.

Signed, _____   DATE _____

The second opportunity for anti-racist commitments includes actions for your business.

Create a list of anti-racism actions that your organization has engaged in over the past six months. Of those, label which fall into the category of individual/interpersonal and which fall into the category of institutional/systemic. Analyze the list for imbalances. Does the individual/interpersonal anti-racism work eclipse or distract from policy changes and institutional accountability?

Does the focus on institutional/systemic racism still allow space or create permission for individual/interpersonal racism to exist? If so, in what ways?

What changes need to be made to ensure that your organization is creating an anti-racist culture instead of just attempting to complete an anti-racist checklist or to-do list?

You have come to the final chapter of *Doing Anti-Racist Business: Disrupting and Dismantling Racism with the 4REALS,* but the work of anti-racism continues. It continues beyond the appendices and after you close the book or shut off your device. The work of anti-racism must continue until racism has been dislodged, disrupted, and dismantled. In order for anti-racism to happen in REAL life, each of us must continue to engage in REAL TALK with REAL STRATEGIES in REAL TIME for REAL CHANGE.

> ### *"We who believe in freedom cannot rest until it comes."*
> **—Sweet Honey in the Rock**

> ### *"Freedom cannot be until racism is no more."*
> **—4REALS LLC**

Appendix A

Real Time Scenarios: Authors' Responses

Scenario 1: *An Asian woman attends a town hall meeting gathered to discuss ways to "create organizational unity." The discussion moves to COVID, precautions, and the ways that racism has created different health, economic, and social consequences of COVID based in racial identity. Hearing this, she specifically highlights the term "Chinese virus" as harmful and racist. She shares experiences of her own and those of her children and how isolated they feel from their community that once embraced them. She also mentions how she doesn't always know how she "fits" within conversations about racism that only talk about "Black and white."*

<u>Example response:</u>

Racism in any of its forms is always wrong. That you and your family have been the direct and indirect targets of racism is unacceptable. We must be willing and capable of shutting down all racial slurs, including but not limited to the one you just mentioned, which falsely blames China and Chinese people for COVID. Anti-Black racism, Anti-Asian or Anti-Pacific Islander racism, and all other forms of racism are based in white supremacy, which pits BIPAL people against each other to avoid addressing the real injustices and oppression of racism. As a company, we can be responsible only when we refuse to allow any racism or racialized prejudice to harm any BIPAL person.

Scenario 2: *At an anti-racism rally, a number of leaders of social justice and other nonprofit organizations were invited to speak. A white male president of a national social justice organization was one of the speakers. He had a wide range of accomplishments on his resume and in his work as president leading a coalition made up of diverse ideologies to work together. However, he had no proven or documented evidence of anti-racism work to his credit—either vocational or personal. His speech invited all gathered to rely on love to unify us, cautioned against focusing on our differences, and highlighted exemplary people of color who have done the work of bringing people together in the face of hatred, including the Rev. Dr. Martin Luther King Jr.*

Example responses:

1. Organize a chant to disrupt speech in REAL TIME:

   a. "Racism isn't interrupted by love alone!"

   b. "Some of the worst racism is perpetrated by white moderates!" (This is based on the Rev. Dr. Martin Luther King Jr.'s *Letter from Birmingham Jail.*)

   c. "Unity doesn't equal equity!"

   d. "Racial justice requires anti-racism!"

   e. "Justice is what love looks like in public!" (This is from Dr. Cornel West.)

2. Use social media to amplify the event's hashtag and add critiques of the "unity and love" message, which cannot interrupt and dismantle racism.

3. Write opinion pieces for papers, blogs, Medium, academia, and social media feeds that critique the model of "love and unity," which attempts to ignore or erase the realities of racism. Include five specific anti-racism strategies found in Appendix B instead. (Here is one way you can cite this book as a source: Beckford, Sheila M., and E. Michelle Ledder. *Doing Anti-Racist Business: Disrupting and Dismantling Racism with the 4REALS.* Nashville: Chalice Press, 2023.)

4. Contact the organizers of the event. Challenge them to rewrite their procedures and practices for speaker invitations to include requirements for proven evidence of anti-racism work and outcomes (not just social justice work in general) that must be fulfilled for a person to be invited to speak about anti-racism or to address racism.

5. Contact the speaker. Tell him your concerns about "love and unity" being a method and message that does not lead to interrupting and dismantling racism.

Scenario 3: *A well-known organization tapped four of their employees to represent their company at an annual meeting. The flier was distributed via social media and other venues. The description next to each employee's name and picture, except for the Pacific Islander woman, included their official title and function within the company (for example, Director of Personnel FIRST NAME LAST NAME). The Pacific Islander woman's information listed her name and her marital status as her title (Mrs. FIRST NAME LAST NAME) even though she was selected specifically for her skill set based on her role in the company.*

Example response:

Dear [NAME],

There are four people listed on this flier. All have been listed with their positions within the company except for [TITLE FIRST NAME LAST NAME], who is a Pacific Islander person. She is listed on this flier with the title *Mrs.*, as if you tapped her to speak about marriage and not to share the expertise she has to offer in her role as [POSITION]. She has been chosen to present because of her proficiency in her role in the company.

Please remove this post and retract the flier from other social media platforms, redo the flier, and repost it. Please also offer [TITLE FIRST NAME LAST NAME] an apology for the racist and sexist nature of the flier.

Scenario 4: *A keynote speaker (or high-level executive) says something racist during their presentation (or report/meeting), or someone tells a racist joke.*

Response 1:

Walk out.

Response 2:

During the report/meeting interrupt the speaker (high-level executive):

- "I will need to interrupt you, (SIR, MADAM, TITLE). Your wording is inappropriate."

- "Your wording is unacceptable. I will not cosign your racism by allowing it to continue."

- Specifically for high-level executive speakers: "You, (as TITLE), are responsible for the ethos of this company, and you are setting a poor example by using racist language (or logic)."

Response 3:

Interrupt the speaker or joke teller.

- "No, (Sir, Ma'am). That's racist."

- "You are out of order."

Response 4:

"Wait! That was a racist comment. You owe all of us sitting here an apology."

Response 5:

"As the organizer for this event, I must interject and inform you that your last statement was racist and derogatory. Please apologize to the guests who are here. We will resume our program. The next person up to the mic is [NAME]."

Response 6:

"I'm going to interrupt you right there. The punchline of this joke is relying/ will rely on racism, and that is unacceptable. You should apologize for telling it."

Appendix B

LIST OF STRATEGIES

The following is a list of 180 strategies, anti-racist ideas, and ACTION-NOW Learning Engagements that can be used right away. Use the prompt below, the page number(s) associated with it, and the interpretive question "How can I use this to interrupt and dismantle racism?" to enact anti-racism by engaging in REAL TALK with REAL STRATEGIES in REAL TIME for REAL CHANGE.

1.   Interrogate your assumptions about leaders' (business, social justice, nonprofit, or otherwise) willingness, commitment to, and abilities for anti-racism work. (Introduction, p. 2)

2.   How have you refuted the lie that colorblindness ("I don't see color") is anti-racist? (Introduction, p. 5)

3.   How have your actions reflected the reality that more talk promotes harm, while REAL TALK interrupts harm? (Introduction, p. 5)

4.   For white people: Use the phrase "for those of us who are white" to avoid trying to separate us from our whiteness and from "those other white people," or trying to pretend that we are somehow outside of the system of racism even while we do anti-racism work. (Introduction, p. 6)

5.   White people: Reduce our talking time and our need for others to pay attention to our experiences, feelings, and strategies. (Introduction, p. 6)

6.   Avoid "workshop hoarding" that collects information about anti-racism instead of doing the work of anti-racism. (Introduction, p. 6, and REAL STRATEGIES, p. 41)

7.   Correct the misinterpretation of the "address the wrong-doer in private" story and teach how responsible interpretations do the work of anti-racism (Introduction, pp. 7-9)

8.   Only do role-playing scenarios that depict the interruption of the racism, not the racism itself. (Introduction, p. 9, and REAL TIME, pp. 65-66, for fuller description)

9. Create and utilize anti-racist pledges in general and interrogation questions. (ACTION-NOW Learning Engagement, pp. 15-17)

10. Assume humanity and build trust. (Introduction, Anti-Racist Pledge, p. 17)

11. Do anti-racism work based in racial positionality and take on associated challenges. (Anti-Racist Pledge, p. 17, and REAL STRATEGIES, pp. 48-49)

12. Recognize and avoid using "good-sounding words" that actually do harm. (Anti-Racist Pledge, p. 17)

13. Evaluate your (or your organization's) no-tolerance policy regarding violence. Determine how racism is or is not considered violence in terms of the policy or stance. (REAL TALK, pp. 19-20)

14. In terms of racism and anti-racism, what is "the talk?" In what ways can it replicate racism, and in what ways can it repudiate racism? (REAL TALK, pp. 21-22)

15. For white people: Eliminate all uses of white protective silence. For BIPAL people: Eliminate the need to respond to demands for speech or to make excuses for white protective silence. (REAL TALK, pp. 22-25)

16. Ensure that you use and understand the phrase "silence is violence" in ways that do anti-racism work and do not perpetrate racism. (REAL TALK, pp. 25-27)

17. For white people: Interrupt racism in the midst of the meeting. (REAL TALK, p. 28)

18. Refuse to offer "thoughts and prayers" without any substantial and concrete measures of anti-racist action accompanying them. (REAL TALK, pp. 28-29)

19. Refuse to protect white people from the discomfort of addressing racism or from the consequences of co-opting anti-racism strategies like "silence is violence." (REAL TALK, p. 30)

20. Engage in anti-racist righteous silence. (REAL TALK, ACTION-NOW Learning Engagement, p. 32)

21. Engage in the anti-racist silence of learning. (REAL TALK, ACTION-NOW Learning Engagement, p. 33)

22. For BIPAL people: Engage in anti-racist protective silence. (REAL TALK, ACTION-NOW Learning Engagement, p. 34)

23. For white people: Refuse to engage in racist protective silence (REAL TALK, ACTION-NOW Learning Engagement, p. 34)

24. Review all legal, procedural, and best practices language and policies for coded language that protects and entrenches racism. (REAL TALK, ACTION-NOW Learning Engagement, p. 36)

25. Identify the language that silences and omits the factors of systemic racism that create and sustain racial inequities. (REAL TALK, ACTION-NOW Learning Engagement, p. 36)

26. For BIPAL people: Create language and expose the specific ways that underlying systemic racism negatively and unequally burdens and harms BIPAL people and organizations. (REAL TALK, ACTION-NOW Learning Engagement, p. 36)

27. For white people: Unlearn the word *share* when redistributing money to enact racialized economic equity. Remember the phrase "You can't share what you steal." (REAL TALK, ACTION-NOW Learning Engagement, p. 36)

28. Focus efforts on and ensure outcomes of racial equity, not racial equality. (REAL TALK, ACTION-NOW Learning Engagement, p. 37)

29. Prioritize racial justice over "order," "tradition," "best practices," or "standards." (REAL TALK, ACTION-NOW Learning Engagement, p. 37)

30. Focus on structural racism, not the symptoms of racism, which often get us caught up in never-ending strategy sessions. (REAL TALK, ACTION-NOW Learning Engagement, p. 37)

31. Unlearn the word *forgive* for debt incurred based in white supremacist policies and practices. Use and enact the words *reparations* and *redistribution* instead. (REAL TALK, ACTION-NOW Learning Engagement, p. 37)

32. Challenge all policies that pressure BIPAL people to conform to and to internalize beauty standards of whiteness, which uphold racism. (REAL TALK, ACTION-NOW Learning Engagement, p. 38)

33. For white people: Research, learn, and develop the skill set to identify company or organization descriptions that uphold white supremacy and racism. (REAL TALK, ACTION-NOW Learning Engagement, p. 38 action item and representative example to use for practice)

34. Disrupt white overtalking. (REAL TALK, ACTION-NOW Learning Engagement, p. 39)

35. For white people: Interrogate desire for burdening BIPAL people to teach us more anti-racism information. Interrogate need for more anti-racism information before anti-racist action. (REAL STRATEGIES, pp. 41-42)

36. Think about and use "entry points" instead of journey language in anti-racism work. (REAL STRATEGIES, pp. 42-43)

37. For white people: Interrogate and remove all excuses for not doing the work of anti-racism right now. Ask, "What forms of racism still benefit me by this/that excuse?" and eliminate that. (REAL STRATEGIES, pp. 43-45)

38. For white people: Refuse to distance ourselves from our whiteness, the privileges we receive from racism, and the reality that we can't get from our whiteness to anti-racism work without external intervention of some sort. (REAL STRATEGIES, Michelle's Real Talk, p. 46)

39. Use to-do and not-to-do lists to enact anti-racism. Discern and refuse to enact the ways in which to-do and not-to-do lists perpetrate racism. (REAL STRATEGIES, pp. 46-47)

40. Interrogate responses to the wording, "white people doing the least amount of damage and racism" versus "white people doing the greatest amount of good in terms of anti-racism work." (REAL STRATEGIES, box, p. 47)

41. For white people: Build resilience against white manipulation (fragility). (REAL STRATEGIES, p. 49, and ACTION-NOW Learning Engagement, p. 57)

42. For BIPAL people: Recognize when resilience is needed, but build more and more resistance to white supremacy and racism. (REAL STRATEGIES, pp. 49-50)

43. Continually refute whitewashed history and testimonials that center and valorize white people, diminish and erase BIPAL people, and use codes to hide the realities of racism in all of its forms. (REAL STRATEGIES, pp. 50-51)

44. For BIPAL people: Interrogate your involvement in (through witnessing, participating, or urging) actions that perpetrated racialized harm against another BIPAL person. What did you gain or lose by doing so? What anti-racist act will you engage in next time? (REAL STRATEGIES, response box, p. 52)

45. For white people: Interrogate emotional, intellectual, and physical responses to being instructed not to participate in an aspect of anti-racism, a meeting, a group, or a strategy session. What aspect of racism or white supremacy is connected to that? What do you need to do to dislodge it? (REAL STRATEGIES, response box, p. 52)

46. For BIPAL people: Refuse to denounce our thoughts, ideas, history, and ancestral teachings (or to accept white thoughts, value systems, religion, and mediocrity) in order to secure our advancement. (REAL STRATEGIES, pp. 52-53)

47. For BIPAL people: Stop coddling white people's manipulation (fragility). (REAL STRATEGIES, p. 53)

48. For white people: Identify how our white manipulation (fragility) has been coddled by others or by us. Name specifically how these actions perpetrate racism. Refer to strategies for building resilience against white manipulation (fragility) to eliminate any opportunity for coddling to occur. (REAL STRATEGIES, p. 54)

49. For BIPAL people: Refuse to allow white people's manipulation (fragility) to influence which BIPAL leaders we groom, select, and value. (REAL STRATEGIES, pp. 54-55)

50. Refuse to use the crabs-in-a-barrel model to describe the reality that white supremacy pits BIPAL people against each other by using racialized discrimination to restrict access to funds, opportunities, positions, promotions, resources, and rights. (REAL STRATEGIES, p. 55)

51. For BIPAL people: Refuse to accept and obey respectability politics. (REAL STRATEGIES, p. 55)

52. For BIPAL people: Commit to not coming to the rescue of white people when they are confronted with their own racism. Practice how you will do this ahead of time. (REAL STRATEGIES, ACTION-NOW Learning Engagement, p. 57)

53. For BIPAL people: Call out white manipulation (fragility). Do not coddle. (REAL STRATEGIES, ACTION-NOW Learning Engagement, p. 57)

54. For white people: Build resilience against our own white manipulation (fragility) by learning to manage our emotions and to refuse to demand energy and attention that should be going toward anti-racism work. (REAL STRATEGIES, ACTION-NOW Learning Engagement, p. 57)

55. For white people: Build resilience against our white manipulation (fragility) by refusing to expect BIPAL people to care for us while we deal with the guilt, shame, and awareness of our racism. (REAL STRATEGIES, ACTION-NOW Learning Engagement, p. 57)

56. For white people: Build resilience against our white manipulation (fragility) by taking the time and effort necessary to learn how what we do or did is racist and what to do instead. (REAL STRATEGIES, ACTION-NOW Learning Engagement, p. 57)

57. Refuse to allow white manipulation (fragility) to be acceptable, ever. (REAL STRATEGIES, ACTION-NOW Learning Engagement, p. 57)

58. For BIPAL people: Honor BIPAL-only spaces by reserving the option to invite or not invite white people, and remember to give ourselves permission/allow ourselves to be in spaces where we have and utilize this option. (REAL STRATEGIES, ACTION-NOW Learning Engagement, p. 58)

59. For white people: Honor BIPAL-only spaces by paying close and careful attention to directions and descriptions of a gathering space to check whether it is a BIPAL-only space. (REAL STRATEGIES, ACTION-NOW Learning Engagement, p. 58)

60. For white people: Honor BIPAL-only spaces by learning and looking for wording (explicit) and coding (culturally specific language) that indicates a space is for BIPAL people only. (REAL STRATEGIES, ACTION-NOW Learning Engagement, p. 58)

61. For white people: Honor BIPAL-only spaces by learning about why BIPAL-only spaces are critical and how/why white people invading them perpetrates racism and white supremacy. (REAL STRATEGIES, ACTION-NOW Learning Engagement, p. 58)

62. For white people: Honor BIPAL-only spaces by attending if (and only if) invited by a BIPAL person. Speak only when asked, and be especially careful to obey instructions as to what they are asking for us to do or speak about. (REAL STRATEGIES, ACTION-NOW Learning Engagement, p. 58)

63. Do not create false equivalencies between BIPAL-only spaces and white segregated spaces. (REAL STRATEGIES, ACTION-NOW Learning Engagement, p. 58)

64. Do not create BIPAL-only spaces as an afterthought or add-on, or in less-than-desirable or less visible spaces. (REAL STRATEGIES, ACTION-NOW Learning Engagement, p. 58)

65. For BIPAL people: Remember that rest is an essential component of the resistance strategy we must create for ourselves. (REAL STRATEGIES, ACTION-NOW Learning Engagement, p. 59)

66. For white people: Do not create a false equivalency between our tiredness from doing anti-racism work that repudiates harm we've caused and the tiredness of BIPAL people who experience the physical/psychological/emotional exhaustion from being direct targets of racism. (REAL STRATEGIES, ACTION-NOW Learning Engagement, p. 59)

67. Engage in racially positioned and balanced rest to promote the health necessary to continue to interrupt racism in REAL TIME. (REAL STRATEGIES, ACTION-NOW Learning Engagement, p. 59)

68. Avoid burnout and self-adulatory martyrdom—these are not anti-racist. (REAL STRATEGIES, ACTION-NOW Learning Engagement, p. 59)

69. For BIPAL people: Remember that we are the ones who are best capable of creating or cosigning strategies that actually disrupt, dislodge, and dismantle racism. (REAL STRATEGIES, ACTION-NOW Learning Engagement, p. 60)

70. For BIPAL people: Hold white "allies"/"accomplices"/people accountable for co-opting or plagiarizing the work of BIPAL people. (REAL STRATEGIES, ACTION-NOW Learning Engagement, p. 60)

71. For white people, follow this overarching template for anti-racism work: BIPAL people create or sign off on strategy, white people implement all work except that which is designated by BIPAL people for only BIPAL people to do, and white people hold themselves accountable to BIPAL people to determine obedience to strategy and effectiveness of outcome. (REAL STRATEGIES, ACTION-NOW Learning Engagement, p. 60)

72. For white people: Do not appropriate the words, work, or strategies of BIPAL people. (REAL STRATEGIES, ACTION-NOW Learning Engagement, p. 60)

73. For white people: Learn to recognize and name the interventions that have taught us to move from our own whiteness (in thought, beliefs, and actions) to anti-racism thought and work. Act accordingly. (REAL STRATEGIES, ACTION-NOW Learning Engagement, p. 60)

74. Teach strategies based in racial positionality. (REAL STRATEGIES, ACTION-NOW Learning Engagement, p. 60)

75. For BIPAL people: Transfer mortgages, business accounts, and personal accounts to Black-owned credit unions and banks. (REAL STRATEGIES, ACTION-NOW Learning Engagement, p. 60—ALSO SEE creating racial equity model/budget in REAL CHANGE, ACTION-NOW Learning Engagement, p. 61)

76. Buy Black. (REAL STRATEGIES, ACTION-NOW Learning Engagement, p. 60—ALSO SEE creating racial equity model/budget in REAL CHANGE, ACTION-NOW Learning Engagement, p. 61)

77. For BIPAL people: Protect investments, invest in our communities, recognize our economic power, and refuse to undervalue our worth. (REAL STRATEGIES, ACTION-NOW Learning Engagement, p. 61—ALSO SEE creating racial equity model/budget in REAL CHANGE, ACTION-NOW Learning Engagement, pp. 105-107)

78. For BIPAL people: Place value—monetary and otherwise—on the anti-racism strategies that we create and that white people use. (REAL STRATEGIES, ACTION-NOW Learning Engagement, p. 61)

79. For white people: Transfer all accounts, loans, mortgages, and credit card balances to BIPAL-owned institutions, and use our social and leadership power in any organizations we belong to encourage them to transfer their accounts, mortgages, and loans similarly. (REAL STRATEGIES, ACTION-NOW Learning Engagement, p. 61—ALSO SEE creating racial equity model/budget in REAL CHANGE, ACTION-NOW Learning Engagement, pp. 105-107)

80. For white people: Do not transfer money or accounts to Black- or BIPAL-owned credit unions—doing so could shift racialized ownership. (REAL STRATEGIES, ACTION-NOW Learning Engagement, p. 60—ALSO SEE creating racial equity model/budget in REAL CHANGE, ACTION-NOW Learning Engagement, p. 61)

81. Create economic racial equity. (REAL STRATEGIES, ACTION-NOW Learning Engagement, p. 61—ALSO SEE creating racial equity model/budget in REAL CHANGE, ACTION-NOW Learning Engagement, pp. 105-107)

82. For BIPAL people: remember we are not obligated to teach white people about racism. (REAL STRATEGIES, ACTION-NOW Learning Engagement, "Begging/Asking for help in Anti-Racism work," p. 62)

83. For white people: Refuse to demand help or instruction about racism and anti-racism from BIPAL people by interrogating all the words and body language we use in our requests. (REAL STRATEGIES, ACTION-NOW Learning Engagement, "Begging/Asking for help in Anti-Racism work," p. 62)

84. For white people: Refuse to demand help or instruction about racism and anti-racism from BIPAL people by obeying their strategies and remembering that it is never their job to teach us. When they do, it is on their timeline, not ours. (REAL STRATEGIES, ACTION-NOW Learning Engagement, "Begging/Asking for help in Anti-Racism work," p. 62)

85. For white people: Refuse to demand help or instruction about racism and anti-racism from BIPAL people by critically assessing our language through the perspective of someone who is harmed by the injustice we want to learn about. Would we recoil if an abuser asked the person they abused for help using the same language we're using for our request? (REAL STRATEGIES, ACTION-NOW Learning Engagement, "Begging/ Asking for help in Anti-Racism work," p. 62)

86. For BIPAL people: Resist buying into the white supremacy playbook that pits BIPAL people against each other as if our needs are mutually exclusive and leads us to compete against each other instead of actually dislodging white supremacy. (REAL STRATEGIES, ACTION-NOW Learning Engagement, p. 63)

87. For white people: Refuse to pit BIPAL people against each other by learning and exposing how white supremacy limits resources, access, opportunities, space, and respect for BIPAL people. (REAL STRATEGIES, ACTION-NOW Learning Engagement, p. 63)

88. For white people: Refuse to pit BIPAL people against each other by recognizing how white supremacy often creates separate and unequal buckets for "everyone" and BIPAL people, and that BIPAL people are only guided toward the latter while only white people are guided toward the former. (REAL STRATEGIES, ACTION-NOW Learning Engagement, p. 63)

89. For white people: Refuse to pit BIPAL people against each other by ensuring that information about all scholarships, grants, fellowships, jobs, promotions, and so on are shared with BIPAL caucuses or affinity groups in addition to what is considered "mainstream." (REAL STRATEGIES, ACTION-NOW Learning Engagement, p. 63)

90. Rename and redefine mainstream. (REAL STRATEGIES, ACTION-NOW Learning Engagement, p. 63)

91. Refuse to pit BIPAL people against each other by dismantling the lie of the zero-sum game, which insists that if one person or group has some, there is less for everyone else. Amplify also how equality models support the zero-sum game. (REAL STRATEGIES, ACTION-NOW Learning Engagement, p. 63)

92. Expose every way that white supremacy uses wording, policy, and practices to support the lie that white people deserve—and deserve the largest share of—resources, and how this creates rules that keep resources from BIPAL people. (REAL STRATEGIES, ACTION-NOW Learning Engagement, p. 63)

93. For BIPAL people: To decenter whiteness, resist recentering whiteness. (REAL STRATEGIES, ACTION-NOW Learning Engagements, p. 64)

94. For BIPAL people: To decenter whiteness, resist defending white manipulation (fragility). (REAL STRATEGIES, ACTION-NOW Learning Engagements, p. 64)

95. For BIPAL people: To decenter whiteness, resist conforming to white supremacy. (REAL STRATEGIES, ACTION-NOW Learning Engagements, p. 64)

96. For white people: To decenter whiteness, stop saying "I'm giving up my spot for BIPAL people" and instead say "I am stepping down; my staying reinforces and centers whiteness." (REAL STRATEGIES, ACTION-NOW Learning Engagements, p. 64)

97. For BIPAL people: Elect, affirm, and empower our own leaders. (REAL STRATEGIES, ACTION-NOW Learning Engagement, p. 64)

98. For BIPAL people: Refuse to use what Audre Lorde called "the master's tools" to dismantle "the master's house." (REAL STRATEGIES, ACTION-NOW Learning Engagement, p. 64)

99. For white people: Obey BIPAL-selected leadership decisions. (REAL STRATEGIES, ACTION-NOW Learning Engagement, p. 64)

100. For white people: Obey BIPAL leaders and their leadership. (REAL STRATEGIES, ACTION-NOW Learning Engagement, p. 64)

101. For white people: Interrogate our first and second reactions to the word obey in strategy Nos. 99 and 100 above. (REAL STRATEGIES, ACTION-NOW Learning Engagement, p. 64)

102. For white people: Assess the racism and white supremacy behind any resistance to BIPAL leadership. (REAL STRATEGIES, ACTION-NOW Learning Engagement, p. 64)

103. For white people: Resist saying, "I agree with the goal, just not the tactics" when referencing BIPAL leaders, leadership, or strategies. (REAL STRATEGIES, ACTION-NOW Learning Engagement, p. 64)

104. Be able to recognize the tactics the logic system of racism uses to obstruct the urgent necessity and required skill sets to interrupt racism in the moment. (REAL TIME, p. 65)

105. Refuse to say that some people "aren't ready" to do anti-racism. Replace that language with "Some people refuse to do the work of anti-racism." (REAL TIME, p. 65)

106. Learn about how the phrase "meet the people where they are" and "respect the people" perpetrate and protect racism, and be able to teach this to someone else. (White people only teach other white people.) REAL TIME, p. 66)

107. Focus on outcomes, not intentions. (REAL TIME, p. 66)

108. For white people: Refuse to allow our "I" statements, our opinions, or our heritage to serve as cover for racism. (REAL TIME, p. 67)

109. Never allow for white people's timeline or comfort to dictate or determine anti-racism strategies. (REAL TIME, pp. 67-68)

110. Practice scripts for interrupting and dismantling the racism that disparages Black women for speaking up about diversity in meetings, and prepare to enact them. Then do it. (REAL TIME, for white people p. 68, for all people p. 73)

111. For white people: Practice scripts for interrupting and dismantling the racism that describes BIPAL candidates during a job search as "not fitting the organization's culture," and prepare to enact them. Then do it. (REAL TIME, pp. 69-70)

112. For white people: Practice scripts for interrupting and dismantling the racism occurring when white leaders disparage ideas and strategies created by BIPAL people only to steal them and take credit. Prepare to use your scripts. Then do it. (REAL TIME, p. 70)

113. Be able to describe the differences between "calling out," "cancel culture," and "calling in" and how each works, or doesn't, to interrupt and dismantle racism. (REAL TIME, pp. 70-72)

114. Address in public racism that has been perpetrated in public. (REAL TIME, p. 72 and shaded box p. 71—SEE ALSO strategy No. 7, "address the wrong-doer in private" reinterpretation)

115. Practice scripts to interrupt and dismantle the racism that emerges from intercultural competency workshops when difference is erased or racism is ignored for the sake of similarities, peace, or healing. Prepare to use them. Then do it. (REAL TIME, pp. 73-74)

116. Practice scripts to interrupt and dismantle racism that occurs when BIPAL people's testimonials of racial harm are dismissed as "their experiences" or "opinions" and as not enough proof racism occurred. Prepare to use them. Then do it. (REAL TIME, pp. 74-75)

117. Learn (and enact) five things critical to interrupting and dismantling racism in REAL TIME. (REAL TIME, pp. 75-76)

118. Name two ways you will overcome a personal hesitation toward interrupting racism in REAL TIME during the next week. Then ensure you do them. (REAL TIME, p. 76)

119. Attempt writing scripts to interrupt and dismantle racism in REAL TIME using five things from strategy No. 117. Four scenarios are included. (REAL TIME, pp. 77-80)

120. Name at least two things you can and will do to use your platform and whatever power you have to interrupt and dismantle racism. (REAL CHANGE, pp. 81-82)

121. Refuse to interpret BIPAL people naming the realities of systemic racism and discrimination as if they are excuses for limiting their survival and success. (REAL CHANGE, p. 82)

122. For BIPAL people: Be actively anti-racist instead of relying on the fact that we cannot be racist because we do not have the systemic power to uphold or change policies. Practice refusing to do the bidding of whiteness, participate in racist behaviors, or advance the agendas and systems that perpetrate racialized terror. (REAL CHANGE, p. 82)

123. For BIPAL people: Name any excuses you have used that have prevented you from using your opportunities or platforms to make an anti-racist difference. (REAL CHANGE, p. 83)

124. For white people: Name any excuses you have made to literally excuse yourself from engaging in anti-racism work. What will you do to counter these excuses—beyond simply saying you will not use them again? (REAL CHANGE, p. 83)

125. Think of an anti-racism act that you have participated in (or heard about) and identify, name, locate, describe, and explain with proven evidence that racism has been interrupted and/or dismantled. If you cannot, what would need to be different about the action for anti-racism to actually occur? (REAL CHANGE, p. 84)

126. For white people: What proof or evidence can be externally verified of your anti-racism work? Avoid all temptation to include anything about your intentions, your promises, or your uncertainties. (REAL CHANGE, p. 84)

127. Name at least one specific anti-racism action (one that has proven external evidence of interrupting or dismantling racism) that emerged from your last anti-racism knowledge-gathering experience (such as a book study or workshop). (REAL CHANGE, p. 85)

128. Evaluate how many anti-racism strategies from this book (or this list) you have enacted since you began reading *Doing Anti-Racist Business: Dislodging and Dismantling Racism with the 4REALS.* (REAL CHANGE, p. 85—ALSO read the rest of this list)

129. Imagine you are proposing the creation of an anti-racism strategy or culture in your organization. Consider the following sentence: "REAL CHANGE requires a sustainable revolution in policies, procedures, power, and practice." How would you paraphrase this to teach the decision makers what is required for anti-racism work to actually happen? (REAL CHANGE, p. 86)

130. Use this appendix to answer the prompts in the "Real List 4 REAL CHANGE" templates to create action plans and accountability for interrupting and dismantling racism. (REAL CHANGE, pp. 86-90)

131. Stop asking one BIPAL person to explain how all people within their racial identity think about, value, believe, or do something. (REAL CHANGE, 30 Things Anti-Racists Should Stop Doing Right Now, p. 91)

132. Stop holding all people within a BIPAL racial identity accountable for the actions of one person with the same racial identity. (REAL CHANGE, 30 Things Anti-Racists Should Stop Doing Right Now, p. 91)

133. Stop trying to achieve equality when the anti-racist goal is equity. (REAL CHANGE, 30 Things Anti-Racists Should Stop Doing Right Now, p. 91)

134. Stop all forms of racialized salary discrimination practices. (REAL CHANGE, 30 Things Anti-Racists Should Stop Doing Right Now, p. 91)

135. Stop equating the term "professional" with standards of whiteness. (REAL CHANGE, 30 Things Anti-Racists Should Stop Doing Right Now, p. 91)

136. Stop using racial quotas to cover up inequitable hiring practices. (REAL CHANGE, 30 Things Anti-Racists Should Stop Doing Right Now, p. 91)

137. Stop using the word "diversity" to minimize racialized inequity. (REAL CHANGE, 30 Things Anti-Racists Should Stop Doing Right Now, p. 91)

138. Stop stealing ideas, strategies, and work from BIPAL people and attributing them to white people. (REAL CHANGE, 30 Things Anti-Racists Should Stop Doing Right Now, p. 91)

139. Stop equating people who call out racism with people who are "too sensitive" or "troublemakers." (REAL CHANGE, 30 Things Anti-Racists Should Stop Doing Right Now, p. 91)

140. For white people: Stop using the term "allowing" when in discussions or meetings with BIPAL people. For example, "I'll allow you to speak now." (REAL CHANGE, 30 Things Anti-Racists Should Stop Doing Right Now, p. 91)

141. Stop saying, "It's not that big of a deal" when someone names racism or microaggressions that have occurred. (REAL CHANGE, 30 Things Anti-Racists Should Stop Doing Right Now, p. 92)

142. Stop asking, "Was it *really* racism?" when someone calls out racism or microaggressions that have occurred. (REAL CHANGE, 30 Things Anti-Racists Should Stop Doing Right Now, p. 92)

143. Stop hiring people who cannot provide external evidence of their anti-racism work. (REAL CHANGE, 30 Things Anti-Racists Should Stop Doing Right Now, p. 92)

144. Stop creating anti-racism policies that are not enforced with accountability and consequences. (REAL CHANGE, 30 Things Anti-Racists Should Stop Doing Right Now, p. 92)

145. Stop equating intercultural competency (or diversity or inclusion) with anti-racism. (REAL CHANGE, 30 Things Anti-Racists Should Stop Doing Right Now, p. 92)

146. Stop forcing BIPAL people to serve on anti-racism committees without reasonable compensation (such as adjusting current portfolio or adding salary). (REAL CHANGE, 30 Things Anti-Racists Should Stop Doing Right Now, p. 92)

147. Stop creating anti-racist policies (or a task force) without the input of BIPAL people. (REAL CHANGE, 30 Things Anti-Racists Should Stop Doing Right Now, p. 92)

148. For white people: Stop waiting until after the meeting to tell BIPAL people how offended you were at the racism that occurred during the meeting. (REAL CHANGE, 30 Things Anti-Racists Should Stop Doing Right Now, p. 92)

149. Stop pitting BIPAL people against each other. (REAL CHANGE, 30 Things Anti-Racists Should Stop Doing Right Now, p. 92)

150. Stop pretending as if all examples of racism within your organization are the anomaly and not part of a larger system. (REAL CHANGE, 30 Things Anti-Racists Should Stop Doing Right Now, p. 92)

151. Stop including language in your training materials that urges employees to ignore racialized differences. For example, "we're all the same here" or "we see everyone as . . ." (REAL CHANGE, 30 Things Anti-Racists Should Stop Doing Right Now, p. 92)

152. Stop creating different prerequisites for hire, promotion, and salary increases based in racial identity of the candidate/employee. (REAL CHANGE, 30 Things Anti-Racists Should Stop Doing Right Now, p. 93)

153. Stop equating representation with racial equity. (REAL CHANGE, 30 Things Anti-Racists Should Stop Doing Right Now, p. 93)

154. Stop allowing internal departments to conduct racial equity audits for your organization. (REAL CHANGE, 30 Things Anti-Racists Should Stop Doing Right Now, p. 93)

155. Stop equating tokenism with racialized diversity. (REAL CHANGE, 30 Things Anti-Racists Should Stop Doing Right Now, p. 93)

156. Stop using the term "diversity hire" and learn why it is important to do so. (REAL CHANGE, 30 Things Anti-Racists Should Stop Doing Right Now, p. 93)

157. Stop using phrases such as "effective leadership," "culture fit," and "safe space" to cover up racist policies, practices, and procedures. (REAL CHANGE, 30 Things Anti-Racists Should Stop Doing Right Now, p. 93)

158. Stop allowing employees to use racial stereotypes and microaggressions without accountability and consequences. (REAL CHANGE, 30 Things Anti-Racists Should Stop Doing Right Now, p. 93)

159. Stop allowing executive leadership to remain in place without external evidence of anti-racism work. (REAL CHANGE, 30 Things Anti-Racists Should Stop Doing Right Now, p. 93)

160. Stop equating anti-racism workshops with an anti-racist organizational culture. (REAL CHANGE, 30 Things Anti-Racists Should Stop Doing Right Now, p. 93)

161. Replace the term "minority" with the term "minoritize." (REAL CHANGE, Quick Replacement List, p. 94)

162. Replace the term and practice of "diversity hires" with the term and practice of "racially equitable hiring practices." (REAL CHANGE, Quick Replacement List, p. 94)

163. Replace internal equity audits with equity audits conducted by BIPAL-owned external firms. (REAL CHANGE, Quick Replacement List, p. 94)

164. Replace defining "professionalism" using standards of whiteness with explicitly defining "professionalism" by naming goals rather than prioritizing specific expressions of how those goals are enacted. (REAL CHANGE, Quick Replacement List, p. 94)

165. Replace "bad apples" excuses (as if racism is limited to one person or policy) with addressing how experiences of racism reflect the larger organizational culture. (REAL CHANGE, Quick Replacement List, p. 94)

166. Use anti-racism language and logic to identify racist "red flags" in job postings or "about us" company descriptions. (REAL CHANGE, Job Posting Summary, p. 95)

167. Avoid describing employee numbers without disaggregating by race. (REAL CHANGE, Job Posting Summary, p. 96)

168. Avoid labeling the company as "diverse" when the workforce remains white-dominant or disproportionately white in executive leadership and/or board membership. (REAL CHANGE, Job Posting Summary, p. 96)

169. Avoid attempts at "false unity" by using the term "family" or phrases like "we're all on the same team," which flatten or ignore racialized differences. (REAL CHANGE, Job Posting Summary, p. 96)

170. Eradicate racism from the hiring process by utilizing interview questions that allow candidates to provide evidence of anti-racism work or skills. (REAL CHANGE, Interview Questions, p. 97)

171. Train interviewers in anti-racist interviewing processes and analysis to ensure that responses to anti-racism questions are assessed correctly. (REAL CHANGE, Interview Questions, p. 97)

172. Interrogate all explicit and implicit racialized bias within hiring practices as well as interview questions and processes. (REAL CHANGE, Interview Questions, p. 97)

173. Refuse to demand "free work" from candidates to create anti-racism policy, practice, or procedures. (REAL CHANGE, Interview Questions, p. 97)

174. Ask anti-racism interview questions of all candidates for all positions. (REAL CHANGE, Interview Questions, p. 97)

175. Use anti-racism interview questions to assess a candidate's anti-racism commitment, experience connecting job with anti-racism work, anti-racism skill sets and values, and ability to help create and sustain anti-racist business culture. (REAL CHANGE, Interview Questions, p. 99)

176. Develop an anti-racist strategy for creating a more racially diverse board or leadership group. Then do it. (REAL CHANGE, pp. 100-104)

177. Develop an equity model. Start with ten prompt questions and research any additional information or skill sets needed to enact it. (REAL CHANGE, p. 105)

178. Create an anti-racist budget. Then use and honor it. (REAL CHANGE, pp. 106-107)

179. Compare your scripts from strategy No. 119 to the author-created scripts for the same four scenarios and determine if your scripts perpetrate racism in any way. If yes, correct them. If no, prepare to enact them or strategies from them. (APPENDIX A, pp. 117-120)

180. Use the REAL TIME author-created scripts in Appendix A. (pp. 117-120)

Contact Anti-Racism 4REALS, LLC
at info@antiracism4reals.com
for more information and upcoming events,
and to schedule anti-racism consulting or sessions.

WORKS CITED

Alexander, Michelle. *The New Jim Crow: Mass Incarceration in the Age of Colorblindness*. New York: New Press, 2010.

Asante, Molefi Kete and Ama Mazama, eds. "Nommo." *Encyclopedia of African Religion*, accessed June 20, 2021.

Beckford, Sheila, Tiffany French-Goffe, Richard Hayes, Dorlimar Lebron Malavé and Laurel Scott. "Open Letter to Bishop Bickerton." Black Methodists for Church Renewal NYAC. July 30, 2020. https://docs. google.com/forms/d/e/1FAIpQLSflQML5L95LWs3zw5m2CRSSfqxPJKk IINSPQ1bbQWaGSwjyLQ/viewform.

Brueggemann, Walter. *Interrupting Silence: God's Command to Speak Out*. Louisville: Westminster John Knox Press, 2018.

Cobb, James C. "Even Though He Is Revered Today, MLK Was Widely Disliked by the American Public When He Was Killed." *Smithsonian Magazine*. April 4, 2018. https://www.smithsonianmag.com/history/ why-martin-luther-king-had-75-percent-disapproval-rating-year-he-died-180968664.

DiAngelo, Robin. *White Fragility: Why It's So Hard for White People to Talk About Racism*. Boston: Beacon Press, 2018.

King, Martin Luther Jr. *Letter from Birmingham Jail*. Penguin Modern. London, England: Penguin Classics, 2018.

King, Regina, director. 2020. "One Night in Miami." Amazon Studios.

Lake, Philip S. "Resistance, Resilience and Restoration." *Ecological Management and Restoration* 14, no. 1 (2012): 20–24. https://doi. org/10.1111/ emr.12016

Lorde, Audre. "The Master's Tools Will Never Dismantle the Master's House." In *Sister Outsider: Essays and Speeches by Audre Lorde*, 110–113. Berkeley: Crossing Press, 2007.

_____. "The Transformation of Silence into Language and Action." In *Sister Outsider: Essays and Speeches by Audre Lorde*, 40–44. Berkeley: Crossing Press, 2007.

McEvoy, Jemima. "Wells Fargo CEO Apologizes for Saying There's a 'Limited Pool of Black Talent.'" *Forbes*. September 23, 2020. https://www.forbes.com/sites/jemimamcevoy/2020/09/23/wells-fargo-ceo-apologizes-for-saying-theres-a-limited-pool-of-black-talent/?sh=483321b14622

Stack, Liam. "Ben Carson Refers to Slaves as 'Immigrants' in First Remarks to HUD Staff." *The New York Times*. March 6, 2017. https://www.nytimes. com/2017/03/06/us/politics/ben-carson-refers-to-slaves-as-immigrantsin-first-remarks-to-hud-staff.html.

Reagon, Bernice Johnson. "Ella's Song: We Who Believe in Freedom Cannot Rest Until It Comes." Performed by Sweet Honey in the Rock. 1981. http://thue.standford.edu/jacquie/songs/ella.html.

Tutu, Desmond. *Oxford Essential Quotations*, 5th edition. Oxford University Press, online version 2017. https://www.oxfordreference.com/view/10.1093/acref.

Workplace Fairness. "Hair and Grooming Discrimination." Accessed January 1, 2021. https://www.workplacefairness.org/hair-discrimination.